WHAT'S ON THE WIRELESS?

Published August 1989 by Evergreen,
PO Box 52, Cheltenham, Gloucestershire,
GL50 1YQ.

Printed in Great Britain by
BPCC Wheatons Ltd, Exeter

ISBN 0 906324 12 2

WHAT'S ON THE WIRELESS?

by David Lazell

Introduction

In an era of never-ending change, listening to "the wireless" remains one of life's most enduring pleasures. Although there is still much that is good about radio programmes today, this book ignores them and looks back with unashamed nostalgia to those distant days before the Second World War when the medium still retained its pioneering spirit, the *Radio Times* cost only twopence, and there was a distinct impression at the receiving end of the ether that performers were making it up as they went along.

When broadcasting technology was primitive, and studios not much larger than a broom cupboard, performers approached the (immovable) microphone not merely with stiff upper lip but also with knees inclined to knock against each other. Today, of course, we take advanced technology for granted and pre-recording (virtually unknown in the 1920s and 1930s) can remove blemishes before the transmission. Perhaps the traditional British regard for the hapless amateur helps explain today's booming interest in vintage radio, characterised by publications, societies and the painstaking restoration of old all-valve sets. No doubt when, one day, British astronauts unpack their jam sandwiches on the planet Mars, someone will begin to talk about *ITMA* or *Much-Binding-in-the-Marsh*. The great days of the wireless were also a memorable period in comedy, despite the attempts of high-minded gentlemen to iron out all the fun from programmes.

Fundamentally, Britons love knob-twiddling, and the large cabinet wireless sets of past decades had knobs large and plentiful. You could watch the station tuning indicator move across (or round) the illuminated dial, with its abundance of printed station names, most in lands afar off — as it seemed in the days before packaged holidays. There was an indefinable magic about picking up Hilversum, Paris, perhaps even Rome on a

" We won't be able to have the sofa, George—Father's listening to the Children's Hour."

good night, before settling down with the BBC or Radio Luxembourg. Veteran knob-twiddlers will recall the experience, the source of much conversation on the train, tram or bus on the following day. Some of them "caught" stations much as some people go bird-watching, keeping diaries and lists of apprehended rare specimens. And bright little boys solemnly lectured parents as to the need to erect a better aerial if they ever expected to hear *In Town Tonight* without the signal fading. Knob-twiddling was a great British preoccupation and *very* therapeutic. This book, it is hoped, provides a welcome substitute, at least until you find a 1938 wireless set at a jumble sale or bric-à-brac market.

Some people are naturally struck by radio — like my brother who, as a baby, had a large, elongated wireless set tumble from a table onto his head. He is now very knowledgeable about computers, and there may be some connection. As I was born at Mitcham, Surrey, close to the Marconi radio installations for Croydon Airport, my own wireless-orientation may have been inevitable. In any case, my father brought me up on the right lines, sending me to the shops with fourpence, this sum to be evenly divided between getting the wireless accumulator (i.e. wet battery) recharged, and buying a bottle of "Tizer". Being a mere seven years old, I was quite persuaded that the BBC needed that well-known soft drink for its programmes. Perhaps it was indeed kept for the Corporation's hospitality in the temperance-minded days at Broadcasting House. Fizzy drinks are not vitally necessary for any knob-twiddler: a cup of tea will do equally well, only make sure your batteries are up to their task of tuning in to *Henry Hall's Guest Night*.

All ready? Turn on your wireless set; hold the brown bakelite tuning knob firmly between index finger and thumb, and begin turning *slowly* in either direction. Good!

Now, prepare yourself for a really splendid hour or two with "The Great British Wireless".

David Lazell

Chapter 1

Captain Eckersley: 'John Bull' of the Great British Wireless

Great British Wireless owes its origins more to Captain Peter Eckersley than to any other man, Signor Marconi apart, yet, like so many other outstanding innovators, Captain Eckersley is today almost forgotten. Any knob-twiddler of the 1930s or 1940s owed his — or her — radio enjoyment to the great deeds of the Captain, not to mention the practical advice he gave to home set-builders via *Practical Wireless* weekly. This excellent combination of genius and domestic practicality came naturally to Peter Pendleton Eckersley, but he was a Mancunian, and such capabilities are not rare in Manchester. He was born in La Puebla, Mexico in 1892, but was brought up in Manchester, being educated at Bedales School, going on to Manchester University after engineering training at Mathers and Platts. Academic distinction might well have been expected of him, his grandfather being the celebrated Professor Huxley.

As a young man, the future (and first) Chief Engineer of the BBC became interested in wire-less telegraphy, i.e. "off-air" radio communication, soon to be known as "the wireless". At the beginning of the First World War, official British interest in the medium was limited, although the 1912 *Titanic* disaster had emphasised the vital importance of radio at sea. Peter Eckersley joined the Royal Flying Corps, serving as a wireless equipment officer in Egypt and France. Now commissioned as Captain (the rank was to crop up in various articles about his work, in later years) the clean-shaven, well-built Eckersley was assigned to various "hush-hush" projects. One of these focused on the development of a reliable power source for the radio sets being fitted to the flimsy biplanes of the period. His device, which worked well, utilised wind-power for the on-board generator. Working with another first-rate designer, C.E. Prince, Captain Eckersley helped create the first aircraft wireless telephone, i.e. for reliable two-way, earth-to-air communication. Later, he worked with a Major Fuller on a detection system known as sound ranging, this being designed to detect location and distance of enemy forces, using radio. Many of the wartime projects were abandoned on the signing of the armistice: Britain's lamentable record in national defence, until the later 1930s, meant that the potential of much of the wartime research was abandoned.

However, the affable Mancunian knew that radio would play an increasing rôle in British life. He was asked to design the ground transmitter for Croydon Airport, which though at one time little more than a meadow with sheds used by amateur flyers, was now being developed as London's main airport. Among his inventions was a radio system which, for the first time, used a single aerial (i.e. radio antenna) for reception *and* transmission. Known to grateful boffins and operators as "duplex telephony", the system considerably simplified operating techniques, and its application at Croydon Airport facilitated use of a radio set, also designed by Captain Eckersley, with a transmitting range of 50 miles. Of course, aircraft flew at very modest speeds in those days.

Any list of Captain Eckersley's radio ideas outside of broadcasting would be long enough, but he became a radio personality to millions of wireless enthusiasts almost by accident. By the beginning of the 1920s, a growing number of radio enthusiasts were eager to see some national initiative. The USA was already experimenting with local broadcasting and, incidentally, launched its first magazine for radio enthusiasts in 1905. In Britain, the Marconi Company, having experimented in wireless communication since 1906, set up a special Marconiphone Department to develop domestic use of radio. That was in 1922, and by the mid-1930s the wireless industry in Britain employed some 50,000 people, with domestic sales of £30,000,000 per

annum — an astonishing growth rate for so young an industry. Even before a national broadcasting network was contemplated, the Marconi Company opened an experimental transmission station at Writtle, near Chelmsford in Essex, initially doing no more than operating for 30 minutes a week, for the benefit of a relatively small number of amateur radio enthusiasts. Norman Edwards, Editor of *Popular Wireless*, recalled in 1926* that despite their brevity the transmissions were "lapped up as nectar by British and Continental amateurs". Among the various innovations at Writtle overseen by Captain Eckerlsey, now a staff member of the Marconi Company, were broadcast concerts which, though low-powered by modern standards (15 kilowatts), were heard by amateurs as far away as Rome and Madrid, as well as in Norway. The *Daily Mail*, long associated with a keen interest in aviation, proved to be no less an encouragement for radio, and helped publicise the first true celebrity concert on the airwaves. This featured Dame Nellie Melba, and was broadcast from Writtle on 15th June 1930 — certainly a red letter day for the cause, generating intense public interest. Among those who helped create public awareness of radio was the News Editor of the *Daily Mail*, Tom Clarke, whose press radio ideas reportedly included contact with a *Mail* reporter via portable radio whilst the reporter was travelling by train. Today's press and TV advertising for a far more technological cellular radio system merely extends Tom Clarke's perceptions of the early 1920s.

*See *Broadcasting For Everyone*: Herbert Jenkins, 1926

Between these special occasions, Captain Eckersley maintained a sort of one-man broadcasting service and, as Engineer in Charge at Writtle, discussed technical enquiries from the Writtle studio. A few notes apart, the explanations were for the most part "off the cuff", and were widely appreciated. The audience was very small, and scattered throughout the nation. Until the end of 1922, and the beginning of broadcasting in Britain, only *bona fide* radio experimenters were able to apply for an operating licence. Indeed, there were probably no more than 600 holders of the Experimental Licence. Once broadcasting had started on a local basis, many people other than radio amateurs wanted to secure radio *receivers*, i.e. to listen to programmes only, not to transmit in Morse like the Experimenters. As a short-term measure, the Postmaster General introduced an Interim Licence for the growing army of listeners, as well as a Constructor's Licence for those who wanted to build their own radio sets from components bought from radio parts shops. Both to save money, and as an absorbing back garden shed or spare-room hobby, home construction boomed throughout the inter-war period.

The Broadcasting Receiving Licence was introduced in July 1924, phasing out the Interim and Constructor's Licences. By the end of 1924, 1,129,000 Broadcast Licences had been issued; two years later, 2,100,000 — this increase being assisted by the General Strike when, in the absence of the daily press, the wireless became the main source of news information. Whilst a temporary slump in the radio manufacturing industry was experienced in the mid-1920s — a hard time for many people in Britain — business had considerably improved by 1927. A trade publication noted that many manufacturers were experiencing record numbers of orders. During 1927, the British Broadcasting Corporation was created, basically from the earlier British Broadcasting Company.

That earlier BBC was born — some would say belatedly — on the evening of 14th November 1922, with the results of the General Election. Some might comment that, from the earliest days, there was "too much politics" on the wireless! As one might

The broadcast of the Oxford and Cambridge Boat Race in March 1927 using a short wave receiver.

expect, those entrepreneurs and industrialists wanting to make and market wireless sets were a little annoyed at a rather casual approach from the government. At last, Mr. Kellaway, the Postmaster General, negotiated with the supplicants, some six major companies undertaking to build and equip a first generation of radio stations, these to provide programming for a minimum period of two years. Revenue was raised via the "wireless licence", though in the early days there was no shortage of listeners ready to enjoy the programmes without "paying their share".

Given the carefully avoided prospect of "commercial radio" — i.e. with sponsorship — and the shoe-string aspect of early broadcasting, one can hardly be surprised that studios were small affairs, sometimes used as office accommodation when no broadcasting was in progress. Still, a pleasing range of musical and educational programming went out from the local stations, which represented the spread of British broadcasting until Captain Eckersley's reorganisation plan produced the age of regional stations in the 1930s. The worthy Captain, as Chief Engineer for the new British Broadcasting Company, worked under Sir John

Reith, who had been appointed General Manager in 1922: both men were to have an enduring influence on the character and effectiveness of the medium. Surprisingly, Reith is remembered, whilst Eckersley is not — or at least, not to the same degree.

"Few men command such respect, esteem and real affection as does Eckersley", wrote Norman Edwards in 1926, then adding, tongue-in-cheek, "like Sherlock Holmes, he *thinks* he likes to bury himself in a cloud of pipe smoke, and solve knotty technical problems while other poor engineers spend hectic days and nights fault-finding or some other intricate game".

His "pathetic air and ruffled hair" accompanied great technical ability and, as Norman Edwards put it, the ability to "keep on smiling". Despite the pressures of his job — and they never ceased — Captain Eckersley continued his innovative technical labours. Among these were the first plans for a regional broadcasting system, i.e. high quality radio reception for the consumer/listener via a national network of regional stations. In addition, during 1923, he proposed the early introduction of long wave high-powered broadcasting, later put into effect at Daventry (5XX). His proposals offered Britain the option of a twin-wave broadcasting service, this giving two alternative programmes simultaneously, ie on the same frequency, internationally.

Technical experts from many parts of the world came to London to consult Eckersley who, in 1932, responded to an invitation to visit Australia, there to advise on the establishing of a national broadcasting system. His articles in the *Journal of The Institution of Electrical Engineers* were widely read. A radio journalist of the 1930s, "Ariel", wryly remarked, "It is the life ambition of many a famous man to write a paper for the Institution of Electrical Engineers. But it appears to be just a spare time occupation for P.P. Eckersley." So it was, in the sense that this remarkable man held everyday executive and commercial responsibilities in an innovative field of mass communication. Aware of the more than likely problems arising from a less than scrupulous use and allocation of radio frequencies in Europe, he became involved in the organisation known as *L'Union Internationale de Rediffusion*, which he described as a "broadcasting

Wife: "Well, if that's Captain Eckersley speaking, I can't understand a word he says".
    Husband: "My dear, you're looking at the wrong programme. This is a bassoon solo!"

League of Nations". Raymond Braillard — a radio engineer from Brussels and to whom Eckersley was introduced in 1925 — proved an invaluable partner in the allocation of European radio frequencies, though, as is the way with international gatherings, there were plans compounded by plans.

Even so, Captain Eckersley's not infrequently forthright views on the future of radio proved invaluable in creating a framework for broadcasting among the nations, even if radio enthusiasts in the 1930s occasionally complained of odd phenomena like

"sideband splash". As "Ariel" well recalled in 1934, "Before Europe had grown her crop of high-powered transmitters, he (ie Eckersley) pinned down the precise facts about carrier-wave separation and quality. The estimation of exact details of kilocycle allocation and so forth may not sound like an exciting enterprise, but it was. Eckersley's name will always be associated with technical developments *of which the man in the street knows nothing*, but which the radio engineer regards as masterly" (author's italics, not in original).

Eckersley was, one suspects, a perfectionist, inclined to expect politicians with no scientific knowledge to comprehend the shades of technical argument — as perhaps they should. Writing on the Lucerne Plan for radio frequency allocation in Europe, in an issue of *Popular Wireless* dated 3rd February 1934, he lamented the decision to end the Technical Committee of *L'Union Internationale de Rediffusion*: "Those of us who pioneered the European wireless rapprochement are disbanded and our work brought into futility . . . Not even in wireless do we observe common sense." Captain Eckersley did not pull his punches. Radio's possibilities were, he thought, largely left to chance, and vested interests. In a mid-1930s roll of Eckersleyian thunder, he looked for a better future: "One day, a blast of common sense may blow over the desks of our administrators and they will have nothing to do but to sit back and think. They would then see that their job is not to listen to conflicting voices and then make a compromise decision, but rather to see clearly what is best to do for the thing they administer." One can almost hear those in charge clearing their throats and sniffing disdainfully.

When the British Broadcasting Corporation superseded the old British Broadcasting Company on the first day of January 1927, Captain Eckersley became the first Chief Engineer of the new organisation. With his flow of articles in radio year books and hobby magazines, he was certainly as famous as any broadcaster, although it cannot be said that he sought fame. There, indeed, was the problem. When he resigned from the BBC in the summer of 1929, there was understandable bewilderment among many who had followed the technical advice — and career — of Captain Eckersley over the years. Only in 1941 did he explain the departure in some detail, though, in our more liberal times, we may still wonder why his departure became for the BBC a matter of principle. In his excellent and autobiographical book, *The Power Behind the Microphone*, he confirmed that he

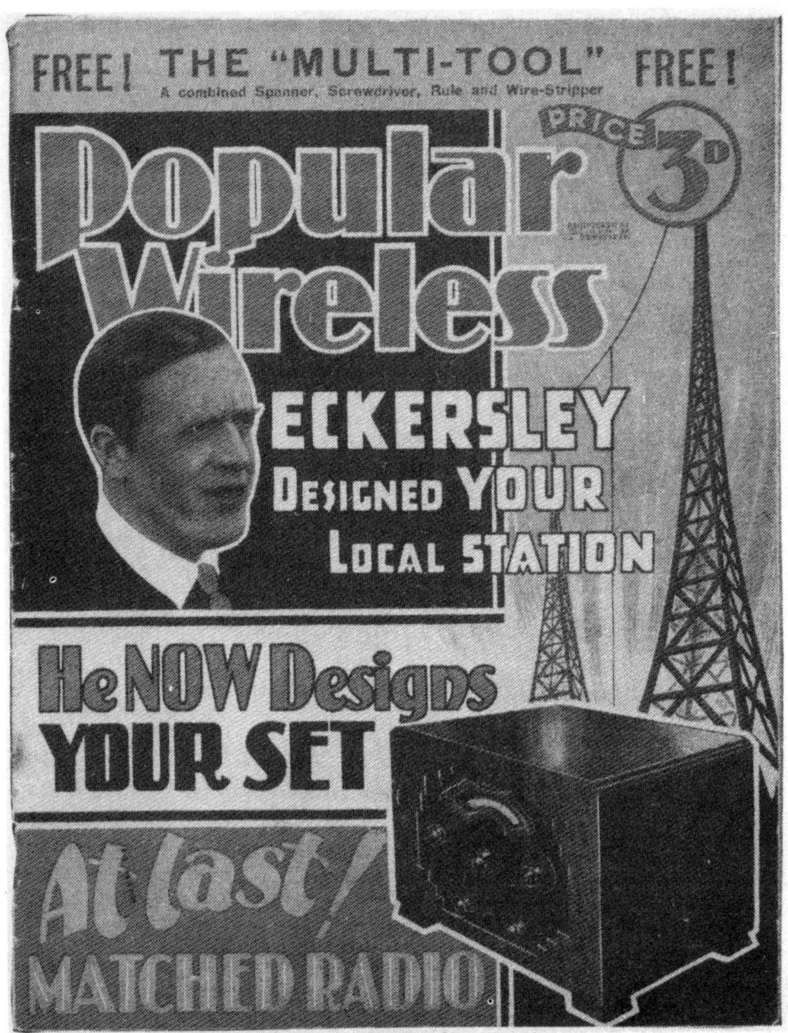

Popular Wireless *was one of the most successful radio magazines of the 1930s. No enthusiast could afford to be without it.*

was "forced to send in my resignation because I was about to become what is called *the guilty party* in an action for divorce". His sudden departure from the BBC received press coverage, not least because others involved in broadcasting, coincidentally and for varying reasons, had also resigned. Daily newspapers, which at one time had even refused to print details of programme schedules, now took a "campaigning interest" in the "up-heaval". Understandably, Captain Eckersley thought that the BBC had "attempted to usurp the functions of my conscience in a matter which I believed only concerned my private life". Some suggested that he was not "sufficiently subservient" for the Corporation, which undeniably had something of a stuffed-shirt mentality. To be fair to Sir John Reith who, as Captain Eckersley pointed out in 1941, "had the right to order my dismissal and the integrity to uphold his convictions", the BBC was still vulnerable to political pressures as an infant organisation. Captain Eckersley might have been "forgiven" had he been less well-known.

Throughout the 1930s, the former Chief Engineer of the BBC continued to write and campaign on major issues. Among his more evident labours (i.e. as far as the general public was concerned) he served as Chief Radio Consultant for *Popular Wireless*, a popular weekly launched by the Amalgamated Press on 2nd June 1922, some five months before the opening of the British Broadcasting Company. Among its other contributors was Sir Oliver Lodge, and in due course the topic of television was added to the title of the magazine. In addition to a flow of singularly well-informed feature articles on radio developments in Europe, Captain Eckersley produced first-rate designs for those who wanted to construct their own radio sets on the kitchen table, etc. A noteworthy example is the three-valve receiver, designed in 1934 to the Editor's specification and using standard components, easily purchased at local radio parts shops.

"It is a set which will stay on the table and give you programmes, not an hysterical, stunted, screaming, fickle puzzle — amusing as is the latter to those who like that form of entertainment," he noted. This was no doubt a reference to less than reliable designs which produced receivers that had to be frequently transferred from table to work-bench. Further designs included a "National Eckersley Radiogram", surely one of the most wonderful innovations from the 1930s. The Captain was also something of a record critic, commenting on the varying technical quality of those 78rpm records. Anticipating the era of domestic

HOPE !

tape recording that flourished (with plastic tape recorders) from the 1950s, he observed, in a 1930s article, that the BBC's steel wire recorder could be used "to give their would-be talkers an inferiority complex. You have to talk — so they say — in a special way, for broadcasting. The principle of the steel wire recorder is fairly easy to understand; to get the machine to make nice, pretty noises is, I expect, more difficult."

The remarkable and ever-inventive Peter Pendleton Eckersley died in March 1963, at about the time that the compact audio tape cassette was being initially marketed in Britain by Philips, and as the prospect of a new generation of radio stations — "local radio" — came into view. His reputation was worldwide: he had been Vice-President of the Institute of Radio Engineers of the USA and, throughout his life in radio, had been a travelling ambassador for the best uses of radio. Many of his ideas

An early outside broadcast from a boat on the River Thames. The interviewer is Wynford Vaughan Thomas.

seem relevant to our age. For example, the use of cable for broadcasting — the object of much discussion in Britain during recent years — was advocated by Captain Eckersley more than a half-century ago. Britain would have been able to enjoy a superior radio service during the Second World War, he thought, had those "vested interests" been persuaded of its practical benefits while, in the 1930s, the nation still had time to build a system based on cable.*

Of the millions who listened to favourite wireless programmes in those first two decades of broadcasting, only a small percentage would have recognised the name of Captain Eckersley. To housewives, children and to most men (apart from radio-construction enthusiasts), Captain Eckersley might have been a character in a weekly boys' paper. Yet the truth was — and is — that much of the wireless magic enjoyed in the nation, and the world, had been shaped by this affable and inventive man. As "Ariel" wrote in 1934:

> "I should like to explain his allegiance to those two democratic ideals, Quality and Service. His aim is The Best, and he wants it for all."

You could say he was the true John Bull of the Great British Wireless.

*An exposition of the benefits and reflections on his own experiences on the cabled radio issue is included in his 1941 book.

Chapter 2

Amazing Characters and Lost Spectacles: 'In Town Tonight'

Following the old press adage that "behind every face, there lurks a story", radio producers proved remarkably adept at bringing interesting and occasionally eccentric people to the microphone. Personalities in the news — comedians opening in pantomime, Hollywood stars visiting Britain to promote a new film, writers, sports champions — could be almost guaranteed an appearance on interview programmes like *In Town Tonight*. A greater challenge was that of finding people *out* of the news, though even street performers, or "buskers", probably claimed they were part of show business. As is the case in so many aspects of broadcasting, seemingly promising projects ran into problems. Take, for example, the case of the reluctant tramp. This endearing fellow was to have been featured in a Boxing Day edition of *In Town Tonight* in the mid-1930s, together with another character known as "The King of the Tramps". In a script reminiscent of modern drama, the two itinerants were scheduled to talk about their experiences on Christmas Day, not, presumably, spent in the Workhouse.

In Town Tonight interviews were usually scripted in advance, using basic outline material supplied by the "subjects". "Mike" (C.F.) Meehan, editor of the programme, worked on the script material, and on Boxing Day morning was somewhat aghast to discover that he had only one tramp — the alleged monarch of the itinerants — and not two. Sometime before lunch, "The King of the Tramps", a certain W.J. Gapes, set out to find a replacement. Fortunately for all concerned, one was quickly found, in the shape of a Jack Phillips, in Oxford Circus. He proved a quick learner in the radio art, and the post-Christmas London press ran an interesting story on the duo.

The show might well have been called "People are Unpredictable". At one run-through (i.e. quick outline rehearsal) shortly before a live transmission, an 80-year-old man still working for a living took a compliment badly. In cheering tones, the interviewer said, "I can hardly believe that you're over 80!"

At this the old fellow glowered rather than glowed, and snapped, "I don't care if you believe it or not".

Another veteran, a Londoner, who had enjoyed a varied and interesting life, volunteered little stimulating material when the script was being prepared. The script editor, disappointed, went to consult with the programme's producer, "Bill" (A.W.) Hanson, leaving his secretary to keep an eye on the old-timer. At once, the old Londoner relaxed and began to recite yarn after yarn to the secretary. She interrupted the flow to enquire why he had kept all these wonderful stories to himself, considering how much they would add to the script. "No fear," he sniffed. "I reckon my life story is worth a lot to someone. I'm not telling my adventures for the bit of money I'm getting for this."

In Town Tonight was one of the most enduring of all radio programmes, continuing well into the television era (1960), including at least one edition in the mid-1950s simultaneously transmitted on television. But, it must be said, *In Town Tonight* really worked best as a radio idea, permitting listeners to picture the people brought into the studio. Imagination is invariably more exotic than real life. In addition television, by its very nature, made demands that might not be met. The 1930s character who kept fish as pets and even taught one to perform a modest somersault would have been expected to *show* how it was done, had cameras been present. Even microphones on their own could be too much for dumb animals, like the "singing mouse" who remained mute while on the air, whilst an equally melodic bat emitted squeaks beyond the frequency range handled by the microphone. But the great majority of interviews were entirely successful.

One or two of the more colourful crises associated with the programme were recalled by the producer in a press interview in March 1937. Lost or mislaid spectacles seemed to be a special

Two personalities from the streets of London who appeared on In Town Tonight — Mike Stern, a shopkeeper from Petticoat Lane, and (below, right) May Phillips, a Brixton barmaid.

hazard at Broadcasting House. At times it seemed as if the programme needed its own optician, as subjects squinted at the typed scripts and confessed their spectacles to be "not strong enough" for them to read the words. Leslie Henson's dresser, John Christie, was scheduled for interview, and was in every sense an excellent fellow. However, he normally read with the aid of a magnifying glass, and had no spectacles at all. Leslie Henson, together with his chauffeur, Jack Walker, and John Christie, were to be included in the feature, but the magnifying glass proved inadequate for John's reading of the script. With considerable speed, a new copy of the script was prepared, the dresser's contributions being typed in capital letters and underlined in red. This failed to provide an adequate answer; then Leslie had a bright idea. He suggested that John Christie pop out and buy a pair of reading spectacles (for sixpence!) at a retail chain store. The result, according to *Radio Pictorial*, was "excellent sight for Christie and a grand broadcast for listeners". This, needless to say, happened some years before National Health Service eye tests! The lack of spectacles (ophthalmically speaking) helped the BBC towards unscripted conversation, rare if not unknown prior to the Second World War. An 84-year-old observer of Test Matches, named Treadaway, was a "natural" for the programme, having a manner of speech that clearly communicated his vigour, both physical and mental. Unfortunately, his eyesight had deteriorated, and he was unable to read his copy of the script, though it was typed in capital letters. Bryan Michie, a well-known broadcaster of the time, handled the interview which was, in effect, one of the very first unscripted broadcasts. Treadaway proved so natural a speaker on the air, that many congratulatory letters came to the studio.

Interviews were scripted for several reasons. There was, of course, the necessity of ensuring the subject said nothing to upset the listeners, although — with live broadcasting — this remained a risk, albeit a small one. Of more immediate importance was precise timing. Generally, *In Town Tonight* interviews ran to two minutes, and even when the subject, or personality, merited more time — three minutes, say — the total number of interviews had to be contained within the time segment allowed for the programme since *In Town Tonight*, broadcast on Saturday evenings at 7.30pm, was quickly followed by *Music Hall* at 8 o'clock. The BBC also had an awesome fear of "mike fright" when, for example, enthusiastically announced guests suddenly went dry. Reading a script could present problems — especially if the subject had left his, or her, reading glasses in the cloak-room — but, after rehearsal, could make the interview seem less exacting.

Some of the programme's secrets were revealed in a 1935 book by J.C. Cannell*, whose work included that of finding the "intriguingly picturesque people" for the programme. Among those featured in the 500 items broadcast since the pro-gramme's launch in 1933 were song-writers and musicians (Horatio Nichols, Teddy Joyce's Band, Choirboys of All Souls' Church, Langham Place, The Dagenham Girl Pipers); film stars and variety artists (Cary Grant, Johnny Weissmuller, Randolph Scott, Merle Oberon, Nova Pilbeam, Norman Evans, Charles Coborn — then a mere 83 years old); writers and explorers (Rip-ley of *Believe It Or Not* fame, Algernon Blackwood, Walter Greenwood, Cherry Kearton, Frank Buck) together with people holding less impressive positions, but nevertheless serv-ing the public. Weather prophets, a woman chimney-sweep, a flea-trainer, a writer of mottoes for Christmas crackers, a cheap-jack, a Hyde Park orator, a puppeteer, a rat-catcher, a riverboat postman — the list of "picturesque people" demonstrated a rare flair for finding talent in the everyday life of people normally overlooked by the mass media. There were, of course, celebrities with serious matters in mind — George Lansbury, MP, Sir Mal-colm Campbell and Prebendary Wilson Carlile, founder of The Church Army, being noteworthy examples. Certainly, BBC radio produced no programme better presenting the astonishing diversity of people living in the British Isles. There was a happy absence of that condescending spirit, or worse, the unconscious domination by the interviewer, sometimes evident today.

A.W. Hanson — usually known as "Bill" — was a sort of fos-ter-father for the programme, though the project had been for-

In Town Tonight published by George G. Harrap

Sir Ralph Richardson, Danny Kaye and Peter Duncan, the Editor and Producer of In Town Tonight.

mulated by Eric Maschwitz, Director of Variety at the BBC. Hanson joined the Corporation as Eric Maschwitz's assistant on 1st June 1933, Maschwitz — former editor of the *Radio Times* — having just taken up his Variety post. A dapper, neatly-dressed man, sometimes sporting a straw-boater hat, Bill Hanson had worked for the Aeolian Company in New Bond Street, London, for a year or two before the outbreak of the First World War. His job was as unlikely as any described in the famous BBC programme, this being involved with the teaching of the pianola to purchasers, many of whom seemed to think that sheer pedal power ensured success. In fact, there were impressive performance possibilities on the pianola once variations of pedal pressure had been mastered. Some of his pianola chores involved delivery and installation, one somehow coinciding with the wedding nuptials of the purchaser.

It is perhaps difficult to discern the extent to which pianola operation prepared a naval officer for wireless procedures. However, during the war Bill Hanson served as a wireless officer, returning to his former employers at the end of hostilities. They were no doubt pleased to see his reunion with the company, which had now embarked on commercial recording. As Recording Manager for the Aeolian Company, Hanson met many celebrities, including Sandy Powell, whose many monologue recordings are collected today.

Many classical musicians performed at the Aeolian recording studios. Among them was Eric Coates, whose *Knightsbridge March* was adopted as the signature tune of *In Town Tonight**. Bill Hanson might well have become one of the leading figures in the British recording industry, but the Aeolian enterprise was bought by a major competitor. There was opportunity enough for him to join the new owners, but he would no longer have the freedom of action he had enjoyed as originator of the budget-price "Broadcast" records. So he wrote to Eric Maschwitz, then about to leave the editorial chair for "radio vaudeville" (as it was then known), and an interview was promptly arranged. According to Hanson's later recollection, Eric Maschwitz "thought I might be useful". It was a masterpiece of understatement.

Eric Maschwitz was something of a legend in his own lifetime, joining the BBC as Chief Assistant to Gerald Cock at Savoy Hill, and involved primarily in Outside Broadcast work. In those halcyon days, a bright young man was not short of opportunity if he showed genuine ability. Whether he was com-

*Among recordings considered as signature music was Elgar's "Cockaigne Overture" but Eric Coates's "Knightsbridge March" from his *London Suite* was the clear winner. Once played on the programme, hundreds of listeners wrote or telephoned for details of the work, contributing to Coates's well-earned success.

Another colourful character from the series — Mrs. Nelson the woman chimney-sweep.

mentator for the Boat Race or telling his own yarns at the microphone, Eric Maschwitz was entirely competent. He also wrote plays, revues and musicals, his best known being *Goodnight Vienna*, the result of fruitful collaboration with George Posford. The film version, made in 1932 by Herbert Wilcox, introduced Anna Neagle to the screen, opening a distinguished and still appreciated film career. Eric Maschwitz had a remarkable flair for studio technology, being keenly interested in the potential of the multi-studio control panel. He was considered "a tireless worker", and undoubtedly needed all his energies when appointed the Director of Variety Programmes at Broadcasting House. Among his "charges" were: visiting dance bands, the in-house Theatre Orchestra, music hall (or "vaudeville", as it was still known in the early 1930s), broadcast revues, musical comedy, and all manner of new programme ideas. Occasional holidays in the South of France, and games of tennis, offered respite from the glorified rush at the BBC. Another great consolation was his wife, Hermione Gingold, an actress equally at home on radio, in films or in the theatre.

In Town Tonight, first broadcast on Saturday 18th November 1933, had an air of spontaneity. There was no long advance rehearsal; celebrities might be met only an hour or two before the programme was due for transmission. The first half-dozen programmes tended to focus on celebrities, these including a "scratch" dance band, made up of famous dance band leaders — this genial stunt being inspired by a surprise birthday treat arranged at the Monseigneur, Piccadilly, in honour of the silver wedding of Mr. and Mrs. Christopher Stone. From the seventh programme odd occupations were featured, soon becoming a very popular aspect of the programme.

A considerable number of people wrote to the BBC offering themselves as subjects, and all letters were carefully considered. For the late-1937 series, for example, some 3,000 letters produced 26 interview spots. J.C. Cannell, a journalist working on the programme, had occasional strokes of luck. Calling in a vet to examine his cat, which had fallen from a third floor window, Jack Cannell found an ideal subject for the show. Strokes of luck also fell upon those chosen for interview. An itinerant street salesman, interviewed because he had rescued, in total, some 26 children from the canal in Regent's Park, was offered three worthwhile jobs after the broadcast: two as a caretaker, and one as a commissionaire. A fire-eater was soon considering the offer of a promising tour overseas. After virtually every programme, the BBC received letters from listeners wanting to contact "long

The team behind In Town Tonight. **Left to right**: *"Mike" Meehan, George B. Fuller, Leslie Baily, Eric Maschwitz (the programme's creator), Mary Sharpe, A.W. Hanson, George Inns and J.C. Cannell. Bryan Michie is hidden behind Hanson.*

lost relatives", etc, included in the programme. Mike Meehan thought that "people like dustmen, chimney-sweeps and night-watchmen make far better broadcasters than 'little' men from Suburbia". In a 1937 press interview, he thought that the former, with only a small circle of friends, had little "leg pulling" to face, whilst the man with business and social contacts might be afraid he had to "watch his words" or put up with criticism, even though it might be good-natured.

Mike Meehan, who had served as a commissioned officer in the Army, was one of the original *In Town Tonight* team, and took on the job of Producer following Bill Hanson's death. On being appointed Assistant Head of BBC Variety, Mike Meehan suggested that Peter Duncan take over the show — as he did with great flair from November 1947. Another *In Town Tonight* pioneer, Leslie Baily, was responsible for the BBC *Scrapbook* programmes, radio documentary portraits of specific years or periods. John Watt succeeded Eric Maschwitz as Director of Variety. Happily, Maschwitz — describing himself as "the

Mrs. Wheelabread, known as "The Chocolate Lady of Kensington Gardens".

rapidly ageing inventor of *In Town Tonight"* — was able to send his best wishes for the 500th broadcast on **26th November 1949**. A 1951 review of the programme published by Wernie Laurie showed recent celebrities on the show — Sir Ralph Richardson, Danny Kaye, Dame Edith Evans, Ava Gardner, Bette Davis, Judy Garland, Somerset Maugham and Carroll Gibbons, whose Savoy Orpheans were (and remain) a legendary dance band, a favourite with wireless listeners. There was, one suspects, a tendency towards celebrities, away from the odd job people and merry eccentrics so finely captured in the 1930s.

Northern Regional's equivalent to *In Town Tonight* was broadcast from the BBC studios in Piccadilly, Manchester, and, if anything, outshone the London programme in location recording. The programme, *Northern Notions*, was produced by Victor Smythe, whose official job title, "Outside Broadcasts Director", seems to have been all too limiting. *Northern Notions* was in some sense waiting to be triggered by the success of *In Town Tonight*. Victor Smythe had collected press stories and notes about out-of-the-usual occupations and happenings in the North of England, becoming convinced that with suitable scripting the material could be woven into a popular programme. In that sense, Eric Maschwitz's bright idea was to some extent anticipated by the Manchester producer. Unfortunately, no-one in authority shared Victory Smythe's enthusiasm for a *vox populi* programme, until *In Town Tonight* demonstrated its real potential. Thus, he was given the go-ahead.

In one aspect, *Northern Notions* was significantly different from the London programme: it used far more location recording, taking a mobile recording van to events of special interest. If anything Victor Smythe preferred to take the mobile recording unit to his locations at short notice. The element of surprise helped avoid the build-up of nervous tension. Mobile recording was based on disc-cutting in the 1930s — those marvellous little Uher Reporter tape recorders, so often used by broadcasters from the 1960s, were still in the future. In addition to coping with the bulky nature of mobile recording equipment, 1930s' broadcasters could face other hazards. *Radio Pictorial* reported that, following successful location recording, Smythe was taking the discs back to the BBC studios in Manchester, having put them on the rear seats of his car. "He forgot all about them when he met some old friends and offered them a lift — somebody sat on the records".

Yet, despite occasional disappointments — like travelling more than 100 miles to interview a wise old character, only to discover the old boy had departed — Victor Smythe's programme was successful*. The items were often reminiscent of *In Town Tonight*, inevitably so. A street musician in Blackpool proved to be a violinist formerly associated with celebrity concerts; a veteran theatre manager at New Brighton talked about his life-long service to the acting profession (he had been born backstage); a singularly melodic budgerigar — who never sang after lunch-time — provoked immense correspondence from listeners with operatically-inclined pets, whilst an interview with the retiring head of the Arabic-speaking community of Newcastle had special interpretation. Adventures of early morning milk delivery men, studio performances by young musicians, reports of artistic endeavours in the North, and reminiscences that would today be described as "oral history" were included in the programme. Victor Smythe had a special interest in objective promotion of the arts to "the man in the street".

---

* In due course, Victor Smythe's assistant caught up with the character, who proved co-operative. Persistence pays!

P.C. Johnson, a London "bobby" at the microphone.

Inevitably, there were occasional suggestions that *Northern Notions* focused almost exclusively on events and people in Manchester and its industrial neighbourhood. A similar criticism might have been made of *In Town Tonight*, which inevitably had a metropolitan bias. Victory Smythe widened the appeal of *Northern Notions* by linking it with the BBC studio at Leeds. Thus the compère, or presenter, at the Manchester studio was Claud Branston, whilst at Leeds this rôle was filled by another young man, David Southwood. Only 20 years old, David Southwood had been "discovered" by Victor Smythe at a Northern theatre, performing in a music hall act. The *Northern Notions* team was considerably smaller than that for *In Town Tonight*, but its members had considerable flair in finding likely subjects, sometimes — it is said — through conversation in Manchester's pleasant public houses, and, when times were quiet, journalists in Fleet Street found some of their story "leads" in a similar manner. Although *Northern Notions* disappeared, along with so much else, with the trimmed-down radio programming of the Second World War, it helped create an interest in local radio, as it might truly capture the spirit of "ordinary folk". One might, indeed, trace its influence on radio — and television — producers of the post-war era.

As a flavour of life on the open road, with a mobile recording van, Victor Smythe's determination to capture on record the shrimp-fishers of Morecambe has special charm. It was known that the fishermen began work very early in the day, and the research assistant confirmed that it would be necessary to commence interviewing at 4am. Richard North, the indefatigable assistant to Victor Smythe, prepared himself for the chore. However, as is the way in location broadcasting, a last-minute check revealed that there had been a miscalculation of the tides. If the recording was to be made, it had to be done on the previous morning. The diligent Richard North not being available for this new arrangement, Victor Smythe was awakened from his well-earned slumbers, and set off. Given his interest in surprising

---

potential subjects, one can imagine how *very* surprised the Morecambe shrimp-fishers must have been!

Although, at times, it might have seemed that men from the BBC planned to interview every member of the human race, there were no bright-eyed characters lingering in grocery stores, waiting to interview housewives on their margarine preferences. None-the-less, all those television commercials probably found their inspiration in *Northern Notions* or *In Town Tonight*.

"*Do you mind if I sit up late, Dad? Guy Fawkes may be 'In Town To-night'.*"

Chapter 3

Birmingham's Wireless: Joy Among the Metal Bashers

Britain's second city has been famous for many industrial achievements, but might be overlooked for its considerable contribution to "the wireless". Birmingham had one of the best-known of all radio component manufacturers, the Telsen Electric Company of Aston, publishers of the mouthwatering *Telsen News*. Radio-construction enthusiasts, banished to the back garden shed, would drool over the Telsen catalogues, published by "the most up-to-date company, the most able designers, and the most efficient radio engineers". So mentioned an advertisement from the early 1930s.

Birmingham was a veritable wonderland for home constructors, with companies like Jabez Bate of Brearley Street, makers of Verona Goods, all British made and including the world-famous Million Earth Tube, costing a mere one shilling and fourpence (7p). In those days, making a good radio earth was halfway between potting compost and inventing nuclear fusion. Failure to achieve good earthing tended to upset the radio valves and tuner. "Utility Components — The Designer's Choice" came from Wilkins and Wright Ltd., on Holyhead Road. Not far off, Berclif Ltd. of Smethwick offered magnificent aerial tuning units which were "much improved in detail and boxed with circuit diagrams". Among other wonders made in the legendary land of metal-bashers were the Clarion All-British Non-Microphonic Radio Valves, prices from five shillings and sixpence. The best thing that could be said of any component in the 1930s was that it was "British made". Alas, there were counterfeit products in

A golden moment from the 1920s, with the Birmingham Children's Hour team. Percy Edgar is just left of the box microphones, with Joseph Lewis and "Aunt Gladys" at his left.

those days, too, out to baffle the home radio maker in his endeavours, unaware that the device he bought from a barrow trader had not, alas, really been made in Brum's Booming Radio Manufacture Land.

The original BBC transmitter at Birmingham (5IT) was a modest enough affair, but its replacement by new equipment (5GB) caused a few headaches to radio buffs. 5IT started over 60 years ago, as an experimental station operated by Western Electric, a pioneering American organisation. The original call-sign of 4WD was changed to 5IT when the station was taken over by the British Broadcasting Company, forerunner of the BBC. This was basically a local station; the first generation of radio stations in the 1920s were local affairs, operated from tiny studios which also served as offices when the microphone was switched off. Catching any kind of intelligible radio signal was a great challenge for any fellow learning how to build his own radio. There was no shortage of tall tales in this regard.

In due course the regional station, Daventry 5XX, offered a much improved service including Welsh language programmes to listeners in "God's Own Country". So, Birmingham — and Daventry — created the impetus for true regional broadcasting,

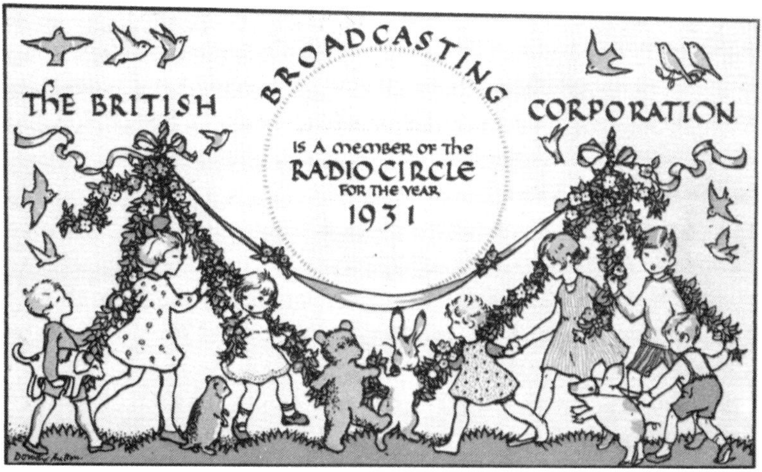

A membership card for the BBC's young listeners' club, The Radio Circle.

and a signal of such quality as did not bend the cat's whisker. Birmingham was a pace-setter in the wonderful world of wireless.

In the early days, staff members worked at least 12 hours a day. The 1920s were the golden days of Radio Circles, when children could have their birthdays announced by the radio "aunts" and "uncles". Birmingham's *Children's Hour* did not perhaps achieve the legendary output of the Northern Regional at Manchester, but it still had some lively characters, including Joseph Lewis, Harold Casey, Dorothy Barcroft and Percy Edgar. The last-named — father of another celebrated Midlands broadcaster, Barrie Edgar — was Midlands Regional Director. Harold Casey — who also helped on *Children's Hour* — was one of the city's true radio pioneers. Such was the interest in broadcasting in Birmingham that television should have come to the city by the end of the 1930s, but for the advent of war. Long-term planning of radio and television facilities was additionally prompted by the city centre improvement scheme. But all that was delayed by another, less pleasant radio enthusiast: Adolf Hitler.

Percy Edgar had moved into broadcasting from the world of theatre. He had been manager of an artistes' booking agency in Birmingham, but the transition from stage to studio was not at all unusual. In the early 1930s, the BBC had its own Director of Vaudeville, whose responsibilities included the selection of those variety performers whose approach fitted the air-waves. Not all were suitable, and there were times when the Director of Vaudeville had to exercise immense tact. The BBC was very strong on tact 50 or 60 years ago.

Percy Edgar — writing some of his reminiscences for *Radio Pictorial* (8th October 1937) — recalled the 5IT programmes relayed from "that tiny studio which was a converted warehouse in a corner of the GEC works at Witton". The shows were "largely spontaneous". By the beginning of the 1930s, the then new Midland Regional station was established at New Street. The station antenna was placed at the Summer Lane Power Station end, between two chimneys.

"Cousin Vera" (Vera Ashe) came to *Children's Hour* from concert party work and the Birmingham Repertory Theatre. A gifted performer, she may have been partly inspired by the droll approach of her two friends, John Henry and Blossom. At any rate, her work for Birmingham radio included character sketches of a young lady, fresh from France and somewhat taken aback at our dafter English customs. Vera Ashe was also one of *The Regional Revellers*, a sort of concert party on radio, a familiar programme format in the early days. Doris Nichols later became "Auntie Doll" on the Northern Regional programmes, possessing a repertoire of tunes that included, "Lilla the Lion Tamer's Daughter". Monologues and merry songs proved very acceptable to listeners.

In Birmingham, as in other towns and cities with their own stations, there were broadcasts by the popular dance bands associated with restaurants and hotels. Also, orchestras otherwise employed in the (silent) cinemas were asked to play on the air. The Lozells Picture House Orchestra seems to have had a permanent link with the BBC for cueing in when emergencies or schedules required. According to Percy Edgar, the BBC at Birmingham transmitted the first religious service to be broadcast. The year was 1925, and the length of the service 90 minutes — which listeners considered far too long. It is also true that

Vera Ashe, the "Cousin Vera" of Midland Children's Hour

Birmingham provided the original post-programme epilogue, a quiet thought before turning in.

No-one should be surprised that BBC Birmingham enjoyed so much talent, for the early days of broadcasting generally had room for the unconventional. Of course, adaptability was essential, as early microphones were immovable affairs that required broadcasters to stretch, stoop or stand on BBC-supplied crates.

Jack Cowper, Midland Regional's Chief Announcer in the mid-1930s, was a former army officer, MA (Oxon) in Modern Languages, erstwhile meteorologist, dance band pianist, and *Children's Hour* Uncle known as "Uncle Jacko". Denis Last, Talks Director, had fought at Gallipoli, and was a former Navy man, one-time printer and sub-editor of a handsome magazine, *The Studio*, prior to joining the BBC in 1933. In those days, local people wrote in to suggest topics for talks and, after due rehearsal, were at times engaged to recall past life and times. Birmingham was certainly willing to reflect the enterprising spirit of industry. It was perhaps hardly surprising that Sir Herbert Austin, of the famous car-making firm, suggested that radio and manufacturing industry had a great deal in common.

One suggestion from the early 1930s was that the BBC should initiate a radio service devoted to the cause of British industry and business, offering not propaganda but well-informed reports on the activities of companies large and small. The suggestion seems strangely topical more than a half-century later, when public misunderstanding, ignorance even, of industry is said to account for many recent problems.

One of the most enduring and popular radio programmes ever, *The Archers*, was, and is, a Birmingham production. Did Dan Archer build his own radio sets in his youth?

Chapter 4

'Barnet's Folly':
A Devonshire Delight

All kinds of wonders have arrived in Devon villages over the years, from medicine show proprietors to itinerant prophets. But, in the mid-1930s, a letter from the BBC had more impact than all of those put together. Going up to Bristol, to broadcast on the wireless, was almost (though not quite) as wonderful a prospect as being invited to see the Queen, and, in this case, the invitation seemed to be an open one. In 1935, opportunity came in the form of a certain Mr. Cyril Wood, member of the staff of Western Regional, based in Bristol. He had been assigned to work on a two-part dramatisation of *Barnet's Folly* by Jan Stewer, to be broadcast on Monday and Tuesday, 13th and 14th January, 1936. At the time little by way of location recording equipment was available, though the BBC possessed some rather primitive disc-recording apparatus which used shellac (or cellulose) covered aluminium discs.

Cyril Wood therefore had quite a task on his hands when he decided to use a cast of local Devon folk for his production. He insisted that every member of the cast should come from South Devon, the area in which the play was set. So, towards the autumn of 1935, he placed a prominent advertisement in the county newspapers, stating that he would soon be visiting the area in search of his "stars". Auditions would be arranged for anyone who wanted to take part in the programme.

The advertisement was torn from the diverse newspapers, and hastily taken to public houses, churches, village halls, and anywhere else where the sturdy Devonians met. "The wireless" was

41

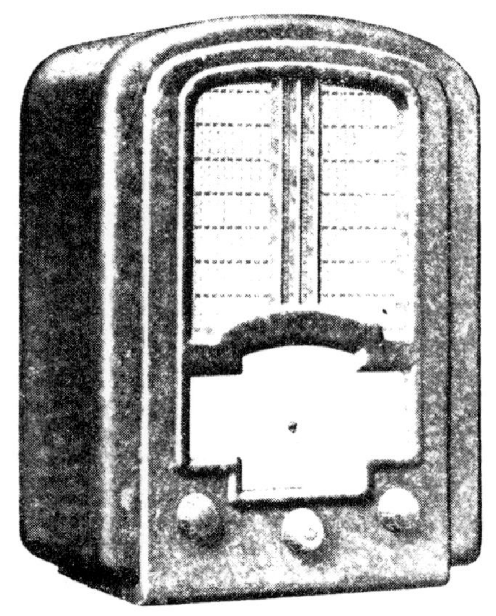

as much a wonder in Devon as anywhere else. But whilst everyone knew what a radio valve might look like, a real-life BBC producer was naturally a somewhat enigmatic figure. In some places the arrival of such a personality would have been akin to a visitation from outer space.

No doubt some people turned up for the local auditions in order to see what the man from the BBC really looked like. In fact, the trilby-hatted Cyril Wood, with his round horn-rimmed spectacles and brisk though genial appearance, might have been a businessman, a friendly neighbourhood bank manager, or even a headmaster. He was determined to secure natural dialect and accent, and was not to be taken in by those who "swotted up" with the aid of the dialect monologues written by Jan Stewer or anyone else. Indeed, he was able to tell whether or not the hopeful reciter before him had unconsciously absorbed accent colour from elsewhere — North Devon, for example. Even those who had spent only a few years away from the area, working in Somerset or nearer "the smoke", could lose that special flavour of speech for which he sought so avidly. Tests were made all the more difficult as his audition sites approached the invisible but, to him, real accent-border between the southern and northern parts of the county. Intermarriage caused some difficulties, too, as maidens from the south had married good fellows from the north, and modified their original dialect colour.

No present-day reader should be surprised at the extent of this devotion, as early in the days of the BBC the Corporation's

"Come up and hear our new super radio."

publications, like *The Listener*, had carried earnest debate on the nature of accent. Alas, we finished up with a standard Southern, or "BBC", English, but at least the debate encouraged sharp attention to dialect — which local radio is now encouraging in great style.

Cyril Wood secured use of village halls, roomy parlours in splendid houses, and public house premises for his auditions. He reflected that three of every four people who turned up for the audition were armed with a copy of Jan Stewer's *Monologues*. As these were available with phonetic spelling, such aids were quite proper, as long as they were not over-used. The 1930s were, after all, the great days of ham teas and other Methodist treats, at which monologues were happily recited by the yard.

Although the auditions required extensive travel — "5,000 miles of auditions" according to the *Radio Pictorial* — Cyril Wood's mode of transport was as modest as his approach. A car, bought second-hand for a mere £15, negotiated Porlock Hill, the roads of Dartmoor and Exmoor, plus other complex terrain. At the end of this Devon trek in aid of dialect, the car was sold for a tenner, which shows that the producer might have been as expert on economics as he was on dialect.

With the auditions over, and the cast chosen, the well-qualified applicants were brought to Bristol via the excellent facilities of the Great Western Railway. They were then conveyed from the station at Bristol to the studios on Whiteladies Road by taxi. In a project which has hardly been excelled since that time, the amateurs were coached in microphone technique, this being combined in a week's rehearsal of the play. Cyril Wood told Kenneth Baily at the beginning of 1936, "In dialect plays, it is rarely possible to allocate the parts until the final rehearsal as, although perfect dialect speaking is indispensable, other qualities do not always accompany the best exponent, and sometimes a promising discovery has to be given an insignificant part at the last moment, owing to nerves and lack of experience".

Certainly, with his "student-actors" made up of farmers, public house proprietors, secretaries and shop workers, the producer had a task of considerable magnitude. Indeed, he faced something of a problem in assigning one of the rôles. But Providence was on hand (it usually is, for such devoted radio producers), and guided Cyril Wood's eyes to a theatre poster showing the name of Bertram Marsh Dunn. In his former acting days Cyril Wood had worked with Dunn, and recalled his flair for Devonshire dialect. A message was sent to the local theatre, at which Dunn was appearing, and the necessary arrangements made. But, with that one exception, virtually all of the cast of that January 1936 production were folk from Devon, hardly expecting that they would one day be "on the wireless".

There is no doubt that Cyril Wood was something of a genius in this regard. Earlier in the 1930s, he had worked on radio productions of other plays with a West Country flavour, including *The Farmer's Wife, Devonshire Cream* and *Lorna Doone*. One of his discoveries was an Exmoor man who, despite lack of formal professional training, took to the microphone with a marvellous portrayal of Jan Ridd. Blackmore would have been delighted, and no doubt amazed! Cyril Wood believed that it was entirely possible to find those with "the blood of Eden Phillpotts", emotionally speaking, in their veins. Such discovery and development of the gift within ordinary people required careful counselling, patience and tuition. Kenneth Baily put it well: "He has put the living dialect right off the soil of the west, onto the air". It was truly a case of *vox populi* — and Devonshire cream and strawberries.

' Which shall we take, the car or the wireless set? We can't take both.'

Chapter 5

John Tilley:
Hilarity in Hertfordshire

Among the great radio comics were those who had come hot-foot as it were from places where Progress was measured in terms of events as exciting as the purchase of a new umbrella for the vicar — always assuming he knew how to use it, of course. The more preposterous the happening, the more it seemed true to life. Styles may not change much over the years, and highly successful comedians like Jimmy Cricket continued to use letters from home to great effect — home being sleepy hamlets like Ballygolightly. Gillie Potter was probably the most colourful exponent of this art-form in the great days of "the wireless". His appearance on the music-hall stage, attired in Oxford bags, striped blazer and straw boater, was as grand as his delivery. He was indeed one of the most popular "exhibits" at the radio trades' show, Radiolympia, in 1933. It was rumoured that the worthies of Hogsnorton had finally agreed that aerial poles in the back garden did not discourage poultry egg-laying as once feared. The BBC stood in awe of public opinion in Hogsnorton and ensured that a report of Coronation Festivities thereat was broadcast on that great occasion in 1953.

Gillie Potter was in the tourism business, and thus a contemporary figure. He was, as he admitted, Publicity Agent for the town of Hogsnorton, which at times seemed to share the same high moral tone of S.G. Hulme-Beaman's *Toytown*. The act was straightforward, consisting of an anecdotal report of Hogsnorton's Latest Doings. This was preceded by a lucid greeting, e.g. "Good Evening, England", together with an assurance that the broadcaster was indeed speaking in English. Radio literature of

877 kc/s REGIONAL 342.1 m.

5.0 A TOYTOWN DIALOGUE
STORY
by S. G. Hulme-Beaman
' The Showing Up of Larry the
Lamb '

Despite the 'showing up', Larry
emerges on top, as usual

5.35 A Pianoforte Interlude

5.45   THE ZOO MAN

1013 kc/s MIDLAND 296.2 m.
5.0-6.0 Regional Programme

668 kc/s NORTH 449.1 m.
5.0   Regional Programme

At 5.0 this afternoon children are to hear the story of ' The Showing Up of
Larry the Lamb '. Note how sorry Larry looks!

A cutting from the Radio Times of 18th December 1931 giving details of the popular "Toytown" programme.

the 1930s seems to have little detail on his background , beyond such helpful information as that his main hobby was "taking his hat off to the directors of the BBC". From his impeccable presentation, though, one would have imagined that the directors of the BBC took off *their* hats to *him.*

The doings at Water End might well have given Hogsnorton some competition, but for the comparatively early death of John Tilley, certainly one of the best comics of the inter-war years, though, alas, almost forgotten now. His real life equivalent of Hogsnorton was a hamlet known as Water End, not far from Hemel Hempstead in Hertfordshire. Here he expertly played the rôle of rural host, thoroughly bemused by ancient tradition. In all probability the local ancients were equally bemused by the comic in their midst. Off duty, at his cottage at Water End, John Tilley looked thoroughly relaxed, and was once described as wearing a faded shirt, old school tie, and ill-fitting trousers that sagged from a pair of uncertain braces. On such occasions he might be doing a bit of work in the garden, watched by his ever-patient wife. A typical day of rural toil included the tidying of leaves on the path, using an old, long-handled broom with indifferent twigs instead of bristles. Any passer-by showing any sense of interest would receive an explanation, this being an excuse to stop work: "This broom once belonged to Medusa". John Tilley

John Tilley, who was once described as having "the gift of being able to talk about nothing for a very long time".

Gillie Potter, who always began his broadcasts from Hogsnorton with a gentle dig at the rather pompous nature of much early radio: "Good evening, England, this is Gillie Potter speaking to you in English!"

would hold the object at arm's length, regarding it much as an archaeologist might consider a centuries-old relic. "It came into my family years ago . . . in fact, not just years, but *years and years*. We handed it down from generation to generation, you know." A couple of leaves would be slightly affected by John's attempts to use the broom once more. "On the whole, we wish Medusa had kept it".

Superb delivery was the secret of his success on stage and on radio. Presumably he practised in the garden at Water End. In attempting a description of his act, a 1934 journalist said that Tilley had the gift of keeping an audience's attention whilst speaking for a long time about nothing in particular. He always found his cottage home at Water End worth discussing. Friends were invited to pop down for the weekend, and there bang their heads on the wooden beams. They invariably did so.

Originally built as a shepherd's cottage, John Tilley's country retreat dated from 1400. Some time close to that distant year, the entire stretch of Water End was offered for £25 — estate agents would today ask rather more for this "attractive investment". "Oak Cottage", as the hideaway was called, offered a marvellous view of the countryside, with trees abundant on the summit of a sloping field close by. In many respects, the cottage represented an ideal for country cottages as described in the popular magazines. It had a tiny sunken garden surrounded by an old red-brick wall, and John Tilley explained that this had once been a sheep-pen.

"So you see," he explained to weekend guests, "I don't count sheep when I want to go to sleep. I count the ghosts of sheep!"

A water-butt close to the front door (which, John explained, was also the back door and tradesmen's entrance) collected rain-water, but the comedian once added some paraffin to discourage some "wiggly things" he had found in the butt. John Tilley's references to Nature's eccentric ways should be considered in relation to the 1930s' press features on stars' retreats in the country, where Mother Nature was definitely under control.

One gets the impression that he was not much into science or technical affairs. During the First World War, his career as pilot in the Royal Flying Corps came to an abrupt end because he proved to be such an expense to the authorities. No-one doubted his courage or energy, but those delicate biplanes had an odd habit of suffering damage as soon as he did anything with them. John was transferred to the Gordon Highlanders — appropriately, as he was in fact a Scot and son of a soccer international who had twice captained the Scottish Amateur XI in great victories over the England team. His real name was John Mounsey Thomson, and his stage name may have been derived from the Tilley Lamps used during the war. On the other hand, it does rhyme with "Silly", though, in real life, he was not at all silly, but often faced with unexpected difficulties. On demob, for example, he invested a legacy of £7,000 in an antique furniture business, the kind of enterprise that would today flourish. Alas, he went in at a time when almost everyone else was getting out: in post-war Britain, there was a surge towards all things new and novel — including, by the way, something called "the wireless". John Tilley then planned a career as a doctor, and certainly showed a marvellous bedside manner. After all, laughter is still the best medicine.

His problems were indicated by a comment he made to someone who asked:

"How did you find your medical exam questions?"

"Oh, I found the questions all right. It was *the answers* I couldn't find."

Saying farewell to medicine John Tilley went into an interesting range of jobs, from helping the Ministry of Food, to organising banking and, later, a refrigeration business. Eventually he landed up with a manufacturer of moth-proofed bags for the clothing industry, the kind of labour with immense possibility for the comic, such as the joke about the man who returned the mothballs to the shop because, however hard he tried, he could not hit the moths at which he threw them. In London he secured work in newspapers, and could have shaped a successful career as a writer on this or that, including rural splendours and country homes. His innate genius at capturing eccentric character impressed many of his friends, and (in one voice, no doubt) they told him to try the stage. He did, and, after an audition at the Windmill Theatre, was engaged as a comedian. The Windmill offered non-stop variety and, over the years, has proved a training ground for many radio comics. John Tilley was an early example of the Windmill Wireless Graduate. With ever increasing demands on his time and talent, John Tilley looked for a quiet country retreat. He was told about Oak Cottage at Water End, and, after he and his wife had seen it, made it their home.

Indeed, Oak Cottage sounded at times like a setting for a radio serial about "country folk". Some of its windows were so small that they might have been planned for an ambitious doll's house. When visitors commented that the roof looked a little insecure, John Tilley would draw their attention to a splendid new length of drain-pipe as the basis for a grand new rebuilding programme he had in mind. Visitors would then spy a small door set in the woodwork over the porch, whereupon John would gravely explain that he had hoped to hire a raven to sit there and welcome visitors, but had been unable to negotiate the restrictions

A pre-war radio advertisement.

of the Wild Birds' Act. Instead, he had gone in for a cuckoo, the loud resident of a cuckoo-clock in the sitting-room. So vocal was this mechanical creature that its cry was heard throughout the area "better than a peal of church bells". It was a *prima donna* of cuckoos and, as the hour approached, John took up opera glasses so that he could watch every twitch of the performance. He seemed to think that it would make a better time signal than all the pips from Greenwich.

In the evening, their sides no doubt aching from laughter, guests were invited to go upstairs to bed, usually banging their heads on the low beam at the top of the seven-tread staircase. Everyone was warned about the low beams but, usually, everyone forgot.

In order to encourage visitors to feel that civilisation had not been entirely abandoned, the spare bedroom was furnished in modern décor — yellow-spotted muslin curtains, yellow satin bedspread and pale cream linoleum of the best quality. Mr. and Mrs. Tilley assured visitors that, as the floors were uneven, the abundance of soft cream-coloured mats had special virtue. Baths were provided, assuming that enough water had been pumped into the water tank, and the bathroom had a window that ran from floor to knee level, plus a very low beam. John Tilley hardly thought the day had begun until, halfway through a morning song in the bath, he had banged his head on it when reaching for the towel.

Weekends at Water End involved a general discourse about cottage beams, as considered by John Tilley. Once a Hemel Hempstead builder was invited to examine the beams, and estimate the extent of the invasion by death-watch beetle. The good man turned up, did his best, and finally explained that previous treatment had rendered any invasion by the voracious creature quite impossible. John seemed disappointed, and perhaps hoped that the beetle might have nibbled those parts upon which he so often banged his brows. Incidentally, such exchanges with honest Hertfordshire folk gave him immense material for his radio work.

Apart from the beams and all, the attractions of the cottage

included a cellar or "coal-hole". John Tilley expanded on his idea for making coal-proof earmuffs for people who had to fetch the coal — but the plan never captured the attention of a marketing man, alas. Presumably, the expansive red-brick fireplace in the sitting-room used plenty of the best nuts. With its light cream walls, dark brown linoleum, large white bear-skin rug and chintz-covered chairs and settee, this main room of Oak Cottage was indeed a comfort to the hardworking comedian. But the décor was a little jarred by the sight of an old school desk, part of one of his acts during which he assumed the rôle of Smith Minor of the Lower Fourth. But at least you didn't bang your head on the desk: shins may have suffered, though.

Mrs. Tilley, a very sensible lady with fair hair and a neat figure, must none-the-less have had some problems rarely mentioned in the press. Most noticeable is the complete absence of any reference to kitchen or cooking facilities. As press coverage was usually written by men, that neglect is perhaps understandable.

Meanwhile, as the visitor peered towards the garden, John Tilley would tap the barometer and expound upon the subject of the weather. There was a very special kind of weather in the Hemel Hempstead area. On the whole it did much as it liked, and completely ignored any advice from the BBC weatherman.

Although John Tilley died, prematurely, towards the end of 1936, he was remembered for many years afterwards and, had he lived, would certainly have had his own morale-boosting radio programme during the Second World War. He was, as a radio journalist declared, a "genius out of obscurity, whose comedy would have kept him a star for years".

Like all great comics, he left a legacy of laughter, based on a philosophy of life and unflagging human eccentricity. Other more recent comics have followed a similar approach, but John Tilley was truly a Great Radio Original.

Asked once if he had any pets, he assumed a thoughtful pose.

"We had a small cat," he replied, "but it left for domestic reasons".

The cat was no doubt fed up with the noise of visitors banging their heads on the beams at Water End.

Chapter 6

The Perfect Mole: Mr. Penny and Other Characters

In these days of spy-mania, reference to any "mole" may stimulate anxiety rather than any sense of enjoyment. The perfect "Mole" was undoubtedly Richard Goolden, whose work for the BBC *Children's Hour* was probably better known for this rôle than for any other. A.A. Milne had adapted Kenneth Grahame's classic, *The Wind in The Willows*, for the theatre as *Toad of Toad Hall*, with Richard Goolden being given the rôle of Mole. Thereafter, he was so often associated with the part — Mole being a cautious, precise and thoughtful fellow — that he played it on many occasions both on stage and radio. Indeed, his distinctive voice in the original *Children's Hour* production so impressed L. du Garde Peach, that parts were written for Richard Goolden in three radio pageants, *The Roads of England, The Rivers of England* and *The Castles of England*. L. du Garde Peach was a well-known writer, whose output included plays for radio and pageants for the Co-operative Movement.

Richard Goolden always sounded the perfect gentleman, so it is somewhat surprising that his first "broadcast" was something of a prank. At the time (1923), Richard Goolden was an Oxford undergraduate, and like many academic young fellows, celebrated Boat Race Nights in style. With some fellow undergraduates, he interrupted the BBC's late night dance music programme at the Savoy Hotel. This interjection into the foxtrots seems to have been more melodic than malicious, a sort of aftermath to Boat Race fervour. Engineers of the British Broadcasting Company were *not* amused, however, and neither were listeners, one of whom wrote to the station management to complain about "rowdy undergraduates". It was a less than impressive launch to a career which included some of the best-loved "radio characters".

Richard Goolden had the good fortune to be at Oxford at a singularly fruitful time for the theatrical arts. Among his contemporaries were Sir Tyrone Guthrie and Reginald Smith, one of the pioneers of television drama. They, with Goolden, were members of the newly formed Oxford Repertory Company, created by J.B. Fagan. In one sense Richard Goolden's university career covered a long period: he once observed that he became a sort of "doyen" for the Oxford University Dramatic Society (OUDS), of which he was for some time secretary. His final performance under OUDS auspices was a Greek classic

Richard Goolden, the meek and mild "little man" of the wireless.

performed in that ancient language — Richard Goolden was nothing if not versatile!

The extended tour of Oxford academia was due to the outbreak of the First World War. Son of a distinguished barrister, young Goolden seemed destined to follow in his father's footsteps, going up to Oxford in 1914 to read for a law degree. In general, the undergraduate fraternity was quick to volunteer for military service — a manpower resource not always valued in its front-line use — and Richard Goolden found himself assigned to the Royal Army Medical Corps. Four years' service included a two-year tour in France where, among diverse other chores for medical science, he supervised sanitation arrangements for the Portuguese Army. On demobilisation he returned to Oxford, switching the focus of his studies to French Literature, and soon joining the OUDS. In addition to securing his degree in due course, Richard Goolden acquired a great love for books — the city of "dreaming spires" being a happy hunting ground for literary treasures. His collection, probably close to 3,000 volumes, covered everything from psychoanalysis to conjuring. The latter interest had been prompted during his childhood, when young Goolden, whilst half-way through a filling operation, astonished his dentist by doing some sleight-of-hand involving a carrot. Another enduring interest was that of music hall songs from the Edwardian era. He had an excellent collection — almost certainly worth a small fortune today — and occasionally performed them in revue. A retentive memory aided such Edwardian interludes, for as a lad listening to seaside concert parties he had prompted anyone temporarily lost for words during a popular song. Like the dentist alarmed by young Goolden's sleight-of-hand, the professional singers were not much amused.

Life as an ex-graduate actor in Oxford had its odd moments. University proctors catching sight of Richard Goolden returning to his "digs" after an evening repertory performance would rebuke him for being out so late. They had forgotten that he was no longer one of their charges though, given Richard Goolden's extended links with the campus, their error was understandable. J.B. Fagan's repertory project proved an excellent opening for

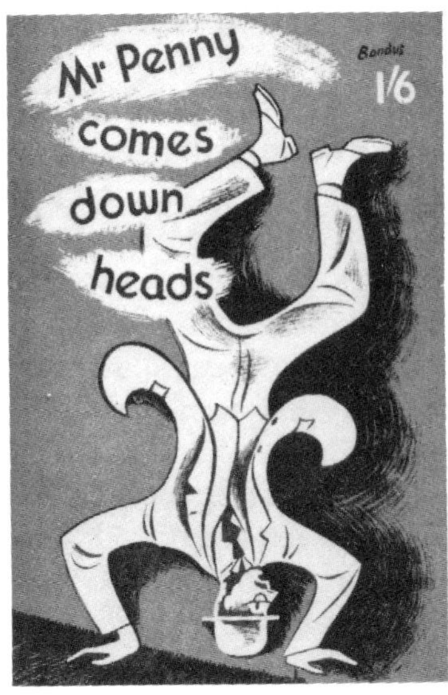

the once aspiring barrister. An early rôle was in George Bernard Shaw's *Heartbreak House*, and he was to perform in its London revival in the mid-1930s. London was reached via work at Stratford-upon-Avon with the Shakespeare Festival Company. But even as versatile an actor as Richard Goolden had his ups-and-downs. He once observed that in a stage career which had included hundreds of rôles, he seemed to have been in many "failures", i.e. performances for which audiences had failed to show up!

Yet the wireless might well have been devised for such a man. From the time of his first (official) broadcast in early drama productions, Richard Goolden became highly regarded. Some of his radio work was heard overseas in the Empire Broadcasting Service, his starring rôle in James Hilton's *Goodbye Mr. Chips* bringing many appreciative letters. *Mr. Pim Passes By* was another success, and, by 1937, Richard Goolden was delighting listeners with his portrayal of that clerical detective created by G.K. Chesterton, "Father Brown". This led to a tailor-made radio part, that of "Mr. Penny" in a Monday evening series launched by the BBC in 1936 as a "serial thriller". *The Strange Adventures of Mr. Penny* involved the odd adventures of a little fellow, presumably in early middle age, in a London office. On arriving home at the conclusion of each adventure, he would comment to his wife, Annie, that "nothing happened at the office today", and no doubt, throughout the leafy suburbs of London, listening house-

Doris Gilmore, who played Annie, the wife of Henry Penny, darning his socks, and (right) Mr. Penny forgets to post a letter.

wives looked closely at husbands who had made similar remarks. The concept of a mild-mannered fellow becoming involved in heroic exploits is a familiar one in fiction. Long years after Mr. Penny's creation by Maurice Moiseiwitsch, television portrayed Hiram Holliday, a character from the pen of Paul Gallico, with similar modesty and innate determination. Mr. Penny was a great success, and prompted a book, a film in 1938, and at least one gramophone record. The rôle of Mrs. Penny was taken by Doris Gilmore, and a 1937 publicity photograph (above) shows Mrs. Penny "darning Henry's socks". A fortnight before Christmas 1937, Mr. Penny moved to Radio Luxembourg, in a programme sponsored by Cadbury's Bournville Cocoa. Successful as the character was, Mr. Penny was in some respects eclipsed by "Old Ebenezer", the character portrayed by Richard Goolden in a wartime BBC radio variety show, *The Old Town Hall.* Each mini-drama episode began with Old Ebenezer's "One night, as I was sitting round my fire bucket . . . "

The genius of Richard Goolden was that of "sheer naturalness": he *became* the characters, so well-suited was his approach to radio. For the most part he did not spend much time studying a radio rôle prior to rehearsals, but preferred the character to develop once rehearsals had started. The technique was singularly effective, and Richard Goolden remained unique. Few listeners realised that his theatrical work had taken him to various other countries, including Sweden, Denmark and Canada. He was a keen traveller, and knew France well, being fluent in the language. On holiday, he often "made up his route as he went along", and was rarely recognised as Mr. Penny, the hero of the BBC. One may well conclude that for "radio character", Richard Goolden was supreme.

Compared with radio in the USA, broadcasting in Britain developed remarkably few characters, though the advent of television provided new opportunities for story-tellers like John Slater and Antony Oliver, both excellent actors. John Slater, as a Cockney stall-holder, related stories about the kind of people who might today be included in a TV serial or soap opera, like *East Enders*, for example. The wireless had one of the best of story-tellers, A.J. Alan, this *nom de microphone* being used by a former commissioned officer and civil servant. A.J. Alan's stories had a sort of "mystery dimension"; one of "there's more to life than meets the eye". A.J. Alan was probably best known in the 1920s, the decade that saw publication of his best-selling story collection, *Good Evening, Everyone.*

Some performers developed their own character-creations, among the best remembered being Jeanne de Casalis and her portrayal of "Mrs. Feather", a well-bred lady wrestling with the mysteries of the telephone. Undoubtedly, the character was born of inspiration. Even as recently as the 1950s, one could find people who confessed that they "did not know how to use the telephone". In the 1930s, when Mrs. Feather first approached the instrument of mystification (the telephone, not the microphone) the situation was far worse. Thus, Mrs. Feather showed that whilst the telephone was hardly an aid to communication, it was not to be feared.

Today, this astutely observed character would probably be adopted for British Telecom commercials. The act consisted of conversations conducted by Mrs. Feather with various tradesmen, friends and relations at the other end of the line, and during which a spectrum of emotions (astonishment, mild aggravation, concern, hilarity, etc) was expressed. Mrs. Feather was a *tour de force*, or even better, a *tour de tele-phone*, and always finely por-trayed by Jeanne de Casalis whose acting career embraced the USA, France and Britain. She was born in Basutoland, one of the then British protectorates in South Africa, and her profes-sional career included music and writing. The latter can be observed in journals of the inter-war period, with her articles on fashion appearing in a pictorial weekly. She wrote all her mat-erial, Mrs. Feather being in the tradition of broadcast mono-logues once a favourite with British listeners. According to contemporary publicity, the Mrs. Feather pieces were based on observations of her friends and of

Scatter-brained Mrs. Feather, the unforgettable creation of Jeanne de Casalis.

herself. However, the 1930s publicity notes that since Mrs. Feather entered the de Casalis household, "she has lost all authority in the home and cannot get servants to take her seri-ously". Jeanne de Casalis was married to Colin Clive, and according to a press directory, "has a delightful little cottage in Kent in which she leads a real simple life". One wonders if the cottage was equipped with a telephone.

Further entirely fruitless battles with progress were captured by Robb Wilton, who was certainly one of the most popular comedians on radio. His superb timing and sense of the "straight-faced" ridiculous added much to his all too rare appear-ances in films yet, like Richard Goolden's Mr. Penny, wide pub-lic recognition of talent came rapidly through portrayal of a "radio character". Robb Wilton's radio work, though excellent, hardly caught national attention until during 1937, when he was given his own five-minute radio spot every Saturday for an initial six-week series. In this he appeared as *Mr. Muddleton, JP*, a magistrate recalling the awfulness of the criminal mind and his wife's cooking. He was perhaps a relative of the "Mr. Muddle-combe, JP" close to Robb Wilton's heart. The 1937 series was the result of his success with earlier portrayals based on his music hall turns, notably that of a fireman somewhat delayed by an indisposed horse and lethargic staff ("Well, can you keep the fire going until we get there?"). Will Hay, another popular comic on radio, achieved noteworthy hilarity with a film loosely based on fire-chasing: *Where's That Fire?* with Graham Moffat and Moore Marriott. Robb Wilton did his act in a British film of the time, using a speaking tube with the same lack of achievement observed with Mrs. Feather.

Mr. Muddlecombe, JP became a national favourite, and Robb Wilton's humour became a great morale-booster during the Second World War. His hopeful if somewhat confused magistrate became a sort of symbol of befuddled bureaucracy (though this was in fact considerably less in the Second World War than in the First) whilst the period of the "phoney war", between September 1939 and the bombing of British cities in summer 1940, offered a period of national retrospection. It might even be said that there were echoes of Stanley Baldwin, the somewhat inactive Prime Minister, in Robb Wilton's reflections of a bemused British public entitled "*The day war broke out . . .* " The wife who asked her husband what he was going to do about it, might well have been addressing her enquiry to the political leaders of the 1930s. A model of stately purpose based on absolute muddle, Robb Wilton reflected an aspect of the British character in dark times: the ability to laugh at oneself. He was a native of that national centre of inspired barminess, Liverpool, from which area so much merry inspiration had reached lesser precincts like London and the south. Robb Wilton invented a galaxy of authority figures which, if not possessed of feet of clay, had probably put odd socks on that same morning. In many ways, his parodying of those "in the know" was more effective, and certainly more truly "funny", than our more outspoken, pointed radio satire.

There were other "radio characters", some long forgotten,

Robb Wilton as Mr. Muddlecombe, JP.

including, for example, Major Blither and Captain Squirt, the hunting, shooting and fishing duo portrayed by Max Kirby and W.S. Percy. At their best they offered fine talents in the service of radio, like the examples given here. Alas, we have no record of the likely result of Mrs. Feather and Robb Wilton's Fire Chief trying to reach each other on the telephone. Such an encounter would have tested the competence even of Mr. Penny.

Chapter 7

Dick Sheppard: A Microphone at St. Martin-in-the-Fields

More than a half-century after his death, Dick Sheppard is remembered by many as a true saint of the 20th century. Not that he would have felt at home in any stained-glass window. People who met him thought he resembled a mediaeval monk and, indeed, centuries ago there had been a monastery at Westminster called St. Martin's le Grand and, since the monks had come to work in fields in the area now known as Trafalgar Square, Dick Sheppard probably enjoyed a special insight into "the community of saints". Trafalgar Square was created on the site of the old Charing Village between the 1830s and the 1860s, and St. Martin-in-the-Fields became somehow symbolic of the Church in the midst of life — not merely at its periphery.

As The Rev. H.R.L. Sheppard, Dick was appointed vicar of St. Martin-in-the-Fields in 1914. His devoted work during the First World War undoubtedly prepared him for his radio ministry. Troops in transit — and with hours to spend in London, between trains — knew that Dick's church would be open for rest and refreshment. Couples could spend an all-too-brief period in the church, saying their farewells. Indeed, St. Martin's became known as "The Church with the Ever Open Door". Long after the Armistice in November 1918, former servicemen remembered the church — and Dick's kindness — with considerable affection. Thus, when Dick became involved in broadcasting he had an almost "guaranteed audience", including very many who had somehow lost touch with church life.

Outposts of Empire
COOKERY TALK

Outposts of Empire
THE SYMPHONY CONCERT

The story of Dick's work on the wireless is truly remarkable. Apparently, John Reith — General Manager of the pre-corporation British Broadcasting Company — invited Dick to consider the prospect, this happy proposal being made over tea at the Savoy Hotel. Dick was prompted to become a sort of "facilitator", encouraging leading churchmen to become involved in religious broadcasting. John Reith's approach was entirely pragmatic: it is unlikely that he would have approved of a radio service owned by the churches. However, a balanced programme output certainly required its share of spirituality. He was right, of course: even in our somewhat secularised land, religious broadcasting continues to enjoy high public regard. Yet in 1924, when Dick Sheppard took up the challenge, the ecclesiastical authorities showed little interest in the infant medium. Dick, for example, thought that radio listeners would be especially interested in services broadcast from the famous and venerable churches of London. Alas, he received polite but firm rebuffs, with one traditionalist churchman horrified that broadcast services "might be heard in public houses by men with their hats on".

Dick Sheppard, whose broadcasts broke new ground and brought Christian comfort to thousands of listeners.

We should not be too hard on these somewhat unimaginative sentiments. Worship was considered a holy and even private experience whilst, in the early days of broadcasting, microphones and cables were hardly unobtrusive. Dick Sheppard, more in tune with the outlook of post-war Britain, hoped that radio would bring the Christian message to non-churchgoers, wherever they were, and whether or not they wore hats. The first of many broadcasts from St. Martin-in-the-Fields was made in January 1924, as Dick and his friends worked to express a positive faith to a nation still deeply affected by the traumas of the Great War. Of course, there was no shortage of people who thought radio quite inappropriate for worship — forgetting, it seems, that the Creator "built in" the possibilities of all-electronic communication on the Day of Creation.

Dick Sheppard's caring approach was somehow sensed by listeners. He spoke in their language — and there was no sign of that "Vocal Starch" that affected other religious broadcasters in those early days. The proprietor of a retail shop reflected a wide public esteem when he commented, in a trade journal: "I always know when Dick Sheppard is going to broadcast. Everyone brings in the wireless accumulator to be charged, to make sure they're in full power for the service". The accumulator was the glass-bottle wet battery which provided the power for wireless sets — we use far handier and longer lasting dry batteries today. In the inter-war period, local radio retailers had facilities for recharging accumulators. My local wireless shop in South East London did it for twopence, i.e. less than 1p in today's money. Services direct from St. Martin-in-the-Fields were broadcast on the second Sunday of every month. To create a further and valuable link with listeners, a magazine was offered on a postal subscription of sevenpence a year. *St. Martin's Review* enjoyed a wide readership, much of this produced by radio. But then, Dick Sheppard never made the mistake of thinking vacant pews were indicative of a lack of interest in the ultimate message of the Church. If you want to reach people, he observed, you must show that you really care for them, whatever the cost.

Given his enduring influence — and his gentle, unfailing enthusiasm — it is still astonishing to recall Dick Sheppard's indifferent health. Asthma and other health problems dogged him, necessitating resignation of his pastoral duties, an event which almost exactly coincided with the transformation of the British Broadcasting Company into the British Broadcasting Corporation in 1927.

The extent of his trail-blazing in a new medium may be seen in his article in the 1929 edition of the *BBC Year Book*. True, the development of religious broadcasting, as foreseen by John Reith, had been largely assured by the response of listeners, and less by the weighty decisions of bureaucrats. In his article, Dick Sheppard paid tribute to the work of the BBC personnel at Savoy Hill.

"The atmosphere there", he commented, "has given heart to

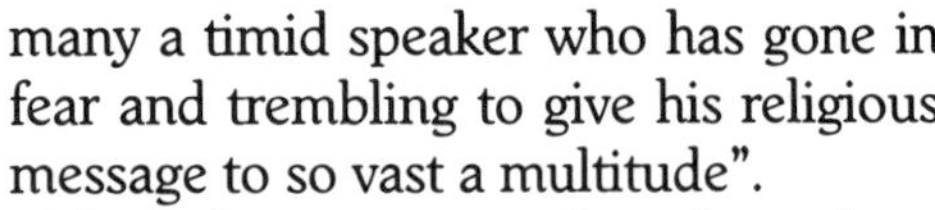

many a timid speaker who has gone in fear and trembling to give his religious message to so vast a multitude".

A daily service was broadcast from the then new Daventry station in the same year, and during the first decade of religious broadcasting Dick Sheppard observed a steady development of this "good work". "Tubby" Clayton, founder of Toc H, and vicar of All Hallows' Church in London, was a popular preacher on the wireless. Father C.C. Martindale spoke from a Roman Catholic standpoint,

The Reverend "Tubby" Clayton, founder of Toc H.

though all religious broadcasting was in most respects non-sectarian. Among well known writers and churchmen, Leslie Church and J.S. Whale could be counted, whilst Dick's successor at St. Martin-in-the-Fields, The Rev. Pat McCormack, proved to be a Christian of similar enterprise and deep spirituality.

Some believed that Dick Sheppard would be appointed to the post of Director of Religious Broadcasting at the BBC, but the job went to another hardworking religious broadcaster, The Rev. F.A. ("Freddie") Iremonger. It must have been a disappointment, but Dick's indifferent health was possibly the deciding factor. One may wonder, too, if so lively an individualist as Dick Sheppard would have found the inevitable bureaucracy of the BBC occasionally frustrating. No man did more to make radio a great influence for good in the land, and on his death in 1937 his marvellous contribution was clearly noted. The *Radio Pictorial*, in November 1937, published its tribute:

> It is true to say that Dick Sheppard, more than any other person, was responsible for the religious revival brought about by broadcasting. In these days of emptying churches, the BBC's religious broadcasts command a tremendous following and among our many wireless preachers, Dick Sheppard was unrivalled. What was the secret of his popularity? It was

The famous Roman Catholic preacher, Father C.C. Martindale, at the microphone.

his qualities of simplicity, honesty and sincerity which shone through that friendly voice of his. It was his gift of happiness which made him love telling humorous anecdotes even in his sermons. And it was his great sympathy for his fellow men which showed itself particularly in his work for the down-and-outs whom he welcomed to the crypt of St. Martin's.

One of the relatively small number of men who could be said to exert a similarly widespread influence was The Rev. W.H. Elliott, who broadcast regularly from his church, St. Michael's in Chester Square, London. Listeners were invited to join The League of Prayer, receiving a small card on which was printed a prayer for national renewal and spiritual strengthening. Every night at 9 o'clock people all over Britain joined in the prayer, becoming as it were part of a great worshipping community. When war came in 1939, the mid-week broadcast services were moved from Chester Square, London, to the cathedral in the city long associated with John Wesley: Bristol.

St. Michael's in Chester Square was somewhat different to St. Martin-in-the-Fields. It was a well-to-do church, with an elevated pulpit designed not so much to assert theological supremacy as to better address people seated in the gallery. Nor did

Canon Elliott look much like Canon Sheppard, being a slim man with a rather lean, pale face and sleek dark hair, well brushed back. But what a great deal they shared in spirituality! In one of his many talks, The Rev. W.H. Elliott paid his own gentle tribute, still owning a power to inspire:

Dick Sheppard died in the house — in Amen Court — where I myself once lived. In that house, there is a room with an atmosphere so happy and so hopeful that I used to call it, "the room that likes to be visited". I gave it that name before I knew the reason of it — which was in part that Scott Holland, that great Anglican, used the room as his study. Something of the vital and radiant personality that was Scott Holland had got into the very walls. You could feel it, just as you could feel a strange unaccountable peace in a little room leading out of the other. That was where Scott Holland said his prayers. If walls could speak, what a lot they would have to tell us of the two men who seem to me, to be among the greatest saints of our generation.

In speaking of a man like Dick Sheppard, it matters little for the moment, whether or not you or I could follow him in some of his pacifist convictions. Dick Sheppard not only preached peace but lived it. He was by nature, a reconciler. Long before he began to speak of the antagonisms that separate nations, he was bringing peace into hundreds of homes. Even that was not by what he said but by what he was. Hatred could not live where he was. It trailed away like the mists before the morning sunshine. Resentments began to look so mean and so little and so futile, just because he represented other things that were so big.

Chapter 8

Christmas on the Wireless: 'How Tiny Tim made his New Set'

Wireless added a marvellous glow to Christmas — that is, a glow other than that radiated by the radio valves. In our more technologically-abundant times, television provides non-stop entertainment, so that we need hardly think about the true Christmas message. During the 1930s, by contrast, the wonderful wireless took Christmas to heart, offering among other delights Yuletide parties with the stars. That broadcast on Christmas Night 1937, for example, included two hours of music, merriment, puzzles, charades, musical chairs and a murder game. Archie Campbell was the producer, the stars including Billy Bennett, Elsie and Doris Waters, Tommy Handley, Stainless Stephen, and "The Two Leslies" (Leslie Sarony and Leslie Holmes). The traditional radio Christmas party was so successful that it was carried over into BBC television in its early days, an annual festivity now abandoned in favour of so-called "spectaculars", and re-runs of major films.

A major event of the year was the Christmas Day broadcast by the monarch, a convention begun by King George V and continued with remarkable sensitivity by King George VI. This was followed on the afternoon of Christmas Day by the Empire (later Commonwealth) link-up, when hearty patriots at the BBC swopped greetings with family folk in the Australian outback, amid Canadian snows, among West Indian seasonal festivities, and so on. Many families in Britain — "the home country" — had members, sons or daughters for example, who had emigrated to these "new countries", and the programme, if at times slightly ponderous, served an eminently valuable purpose. It was

Elsie and Doris Waters, whose "Gert" and "Daisy" characters were originally created for the B-side of a gramophone record, "Wedding Bells" in 1930. They are pictured here with their brother, Jack Warner.

also a triumph for BBC planning and engineering, relating to a range of locations and varying time zones. To meet the latter problem, the BBC initiated programme recording and playback on a 1930s' steel wire recording device, known as "The Blattner-phone" and officially listed as "The Blatte-Stille Recorder". But *that* is another story!

Set-construction enthusiasts were urged to build a brand new model in time for all the splendid Christmas programmes. No doubt many hard-pressed but hopeful housewives were inform-ed on Christmas Eve that their devoted spouses had made a new wireless for their Christmas present. Domestic crises could arise from the hobby: a letter from a home radio-constructor, printed in a late 1930s' journal, indicated that his wife no longer wanted him to follow his hobby, as radio sets, in varying degrees of work-ing order, now cluttered every room in the house. A lady complained that while she acknowledged her husband's zeal in constructing a new wireless set for Christmas, she was never able to hear the best programmes, as he kept switching off the set to make "adjustments" which were inclined to render it entirely mute.

The Query Editor of a popular wireless weekly knew this problem well: there were some men, he thought, who would never leave well alone and who somehow believed that they could obtain stereo, or even television, by changing the valves around and adjusting any wire that looked too loose. Writing in a Dickensian retrospective manner in time for the 1937 Christmas issue, the Query Editor sighed that he had handled well over three-quarters of a million enquiries since taking up the chore in 1922. "The terrible thing about it", he reflected, "is that the radio-constructor is like the Chinese. Start him off asking questions and not only does he *never* stop until he is dead, but his offspring carries on the good work . . . It's the glorious desire to fiddle with the set, to alter this, change that, try the other, that brings the query bag from about 20 to its 150 a day."

G.V. Dowding, AMIEE, the Technical Editor of *Popular Wireless*, observed:

> There must come times in the lives of even the most rabid experimenters when experimenting must give way to listening. And one of those times is, of course, Christmas. Not that the experimenter ever wants to listen: one of the greatest radio engineers the world has ever seen once austerely observed, "I never listen to broadcasting". I suspect the reason in his case is that he once tuned in to *Children's Hour* and was shocked beyond belief at such a childish and irreverent use of the inverse function of pi squared.

A less than cerebral use of the radio spectrum was noted by other great thinkers: Professor C.E.M. Joad of *The Brains Trust* once commented that men of science had laboured long in order that Sid Bloggins could sing *Tripe and Onions* over the airwaves. Friends and neighbours arriving with their good wishes and unsatisfied appetites might also have the urge to interfere with the new wireless set. Mr. Dowding provided useful advice on the ready concealing of the set, and placing of an external on/off switch mounted unobtrusively on the skirting board or window frame. This was "designed to allow the set to be tucked away from the hands of those irritating people who never seem to be able to resist the temptation to twiddle with the dials of any radio set that appears on their horizon". Making the best of this native inquisitiveness among the Anglo-Saxons, a Christmas issue of *Popular Mechanics* devised a game for enthusiasts, based no doubt on "hunt the thimble" or even "the deliberate mistake" on *Puzzle Corner*. The game required that the enthusiasts should carefully examine a wireless set for, say, three minutes, then leave the room, during which time a "mistake" would be inflicted upon it, such as the removal of some small but essential component. Then, the host would invite the boffins back into the parlour, and the first to discover the "mistake" would be given a small prize.

Components from local parts shops were gift-wrapped for Christmas — valves, metal rectifiers, accumulators, battery chargers, even that most useful of items, a lightning arrester (nothing to do with police cars on the motorway). One company even offered to send fragile radio valves by post, surely a remarkable tribute to the postal service. The growing band of short-wave listeners, eager to pick up foreign stations, received encouragement at Christmas too, in the shape of special press guides to broad-

'It's just occurred to me—perhaps there was nothing on'

casting efforts afar off. It would perhaps be amiss to suggest that wireless had its adverse effects on domesticity, but it is true that during the Christmas of 1935 an organisation for the Wives and Mothers of Radio Amateurs was set up in the USA. As a British paper put it, "presumably, these ladies get together for a little enjoyment while their husbands and/or sons are too busy with their radio to recognise their existence". A British branch of this enterprise could have flourished, no doubt.

Despite the unpredictability of the man who made his own wireless set, listening at Christmas was very much a family affair in the 1930s and, of course, during the wartime blackout. In addition to the Christmas Party, the BBC offered an annual radio pantomime, the 1937 broadcast of *Aladdin* including Wynne Ajello as the Princess, Billie Baker as Aladdin, Tommy Handley as a "funny man", and W.H. Berry as "a rival comic". Arthur Askey was also involved. It was, one imagines, not much like Ibsen.

A new musical comedy by Spike Hughes, *Cinderella*, offered "the best twentieth century wit and music", whilst Boxing Day, 1937, included a special issue of *Monday Night at Seven* with "talented young performers". However, the mini-mystery feature, *Inspector Hornleigh Investigates*, written by Hans Priwin and with S.J. Warmington, remained in its usual grown-up format. Dance bands were always featured prominently in the Christmas radio schedules with George Elrick and the BBC Dance Orchestra, Roy Fox, Sydney Lipton (direct from the Grosvenor House Hotel), and Lou Preager prominent among them. Geraldo — Gerald Bright — presented a non-stop retrospect of the past year's romance and rhythm in a 1937 Christmas broadcast with Monte Rey, Olive Groves, Wilfred Thomas and Lily Morris, especially well-known for her appearances in music hall. Geraldo was highly esteemed for his excellent big band arrangements. Orchestral and classical music had a place in the schedule, while the BBC occasionally provided surprises like the programme by Hans Scharling and his St. Moritz Yodellers, described as the "yodel in a musical form rather than a comic novelty".

Carroll Gibbons during his days with the Savoy Hotel Orpheans.

Plays tended to be "standards" in the drama repertoire, rather than work especially written for the medium, though one cannot generalise. The BBC was becoming increasingly adventurous in its programming during the late 1930s. Inevitably Outside Broadcasting came into its own, as roving reporters gave graphic accounts of the Christmas Spirit — and its associated traditions — in different parts of the kingdom. As the New Year approached, these same eager itinerants would ask people as to their plans and hopes for the future — surely a difficult question to answer as 1939 opened. Radio schedules promised public opinion surveys, requiring reporters like Tom Woodruffe to rove "among the evening rush of Londoners and ask many of them, chosen at random, what their New Year Resolutions are". Note the reference to an evening rush: there was no extended Christmas and New Year holiday break then!

The commercial radio stations — Luxembourg and Normandy, primarily — worked hard to capture a large audience for

The Forces Sweetheart, Vera Lynn, who touched the hearts of servicemen everywhere with songs like "We'll Meet Again" and "I'll Be Seeing You".

their Christmas programming. Indeed, Radio Luxembourg also offered a Radio Christmas Party on the morning of Christmas Day, between 10.30 and noon. Few commercial programmes lasted more than 30 minutes; indeed, some ran for only 15 and as each was sponsored by a specific advertiser, it was hard to build up the kind of Yuletide aura that came so naturally to the BBC. However, Ambrose and his Orchestra presented a Special Christmas Gala Programme on Radio Luxembourg on Boxing Day 1937 — thanks to Lifebuoy Toilet Soap — with songs by Evelyn Dall, Sam Brown, and Vera Lynn. Well worth making a new set for! The always excellent Carroll Gibbons and his Rhythm Boys could be heard on the same station; there was probably greater competition between the BBC and the commercial stations for dance band enthusiasts than in any other area of programming.

Sam Costa: a crooner, funny-man and compère.

Broadcasting at Christmas had special relevance for the charities. *The Week's Good Cause*, over the decades a fine channel for that generosity characteristic of the British, was devoted to "Wireless for the Blind" in the 1930s, and later too, of course. *The Week's Good Cause* had its origins in the first radio appeal, which was made by the writer Ian Hay on behalf of the Winter Distress League, on 17th February, 1923. Thereafter, registered charities were able to apply for inclusion in a schedule of five-minute appeals, then broadcast on Sunday evenings at 8.45pm. Among criteria applied during selection was the necessary aspect of variety, i.e. to provide listeners with a varied, if brief, insight into the range of charities working year by year. Once assigned a slot in the coming year's allocation, the charity had to find its own speaker. Dick Sheppard of St. Martin-in-the-Fields broadcast 14 times, usually from the church forever associated with him. Whilst charities often sought a well-known advocate or personality, a child care organisation took the unusual step of bringing two children to the microphone, one 11 and the other 12 years of age. The initiative was rewarded by a response of around £900 though, by the advent of the Second World War, the generosity of listeners had increased to the extent that a minimum of £1,000 could normally be expected from these radio appeals. Guests fortunate enough to enjoy BBC broadcast shows from St. George's Hall could drop a coin or two into a collecting box close to the exit — there being no charge for admission, of course.

Christopher Stone was so ready to help the broadcast of good causes that he was described as "the prince of radio beggars". By his 1937 Christmas broadcast, he had already generated gifts to a total of £80,000, a remarkable achievement. Christopher Stone, a former major in the army and holder of the DSO and MC, is also described as "Britain's first disc jockey" as, in a real sense, he was. During 1927, he wrote to the BBC suggesting ways in which they could better present gramophone records. The BBC, recognising a good prospect when they saw one, invited him to present record programmes himself, which he did with eminent flair. His brother-in-law, Compton Mackenzie, founded *The Gramophone* magazine, and Christopher Stone was its London editor.

Christopher Stone might be remembered for many good deeds, but particularly apt was his presence at a Christmas Party being broadcast by Radio Lyons, this being a special children's edition prepared with the help of Carroll Gibbons, Anne Lenner, George Melachrino and Sam Costa. One of the children, Tommy, assured "Uncle Chris" that he had every intention of becoming a crooner when he grew up. "Uncle Chris" advised the little fellow to sing up well in the carol (*Good King Wenceslas*) about to be performed by the group of children. Alas, the potential crooner took his place, opened his mouth, gasped, and fell silent. The rehearsal was stopped. "Please, sir," Tommy said, "I've forgotten the words". The confession no doubt brought a smile to Christopher Stone's face. At that rate, young Tommy showed every sign of becoming a broadcaster.

Chapter 9

The Western Brothers: Absolutely Unflappable

F red Astaire brought a new magic to "top hat and tails" during the early and mid-1930s, through films made with Ginger Rogers for the RKO Radio Picture Studios in Hollywood. Perhaps that happy influence inspired performers in Britain too, starched shirts and dinner jackets being almost obligatory for radio broadcasters. Among these, Clapham and Dwyer (who had City connections before excelling on the airwaves) had impeccable style. Publicity photographs suggested that they had access to Mr. Astaire's wardrobe, though they had their own joke book. Among the other radio stars promoting impeccability, however, "The Western Brothers" remain glowing examples. Their droll advice to "remember the old school tie", and to "play the game", echoed the earnest monologues of earlier generations, and it may reflect a changing society that, during the 1930s and 1940s, they could parody values once thought basic to national well-being.

Still, The Western Brothers certainly followed today's standard — "work hard, and please the customer" — even if their theatrical coat of arms bore the legend, *Adsum Ard Labor*. They were singularly hard workers: there was a certain irony in their public persona. Hard work, it is said, never killed anyone, especially if he was a foreman. The Brothers poked fun at any number of customs and over-solemn preoccupations of their time — the pronunciation of "BBC English" being a spur to much letter-writing during the 1930s. There were occasional jokes at the expense of "upper crust education", too, with fictitious chums and fellow students being recalled as chaps who could be relied upon to bluff in an emergency.

The Western Brothers (George, left, Kenneth, right) with their "Adsum Ard Labor" motto behind them.

The beginnings of this highly successful act were somewhat unpromising. George had been a choirboy from the age of seven, until (as he recalled in a 1937 interview) "they found out what was wrong with the choir, and appointed me organ-blower. I blew for two years until I got tired of it, and said I'd be blowed if I'd blow any longer." Thereupon young George taught himself to play the piano and organ so impeccably that, by his mid-teens, he had been professionally engaged as an organist in a London church. George was the pianist in the act, and therefore an example to all children and young people struggling with a first book of piano studies.

Church influences were strong in the lives of Kenneth and George who, by the way, were cousins, not brothers. Many members of the family had ecclesiastical connections, a cousin being the Dean of Saskatchewan, and George claimed that he had made his first public appearance at a church concert. Here, in earnest Victorian manner, he had warbled a ditty entitled *Alone on a raft in the twilight*, his shrill soprano voice apparently wishing the raft would be cut adrift as soon as possible. An old lady in the front row was so moved by the performance that, as young George paused to take breath, she cried: "Poor little chap!" This sympathetic interruption in turn gave extra emotional feeling to the moment, prompting the

*The "Chief Cads", as the Western Brothers were known, depicted by "Dux",
the caricaturist.*

young balladeer to burst into tears. He was led from the platform
by a sympathetic Master of Ceremonies, and thereafter went in for
monologues — which were much in demand at turn-of-the-century gatherings, soirées and smoking concerts.

Kenneth had seemingly been destined for the cause of literature.
Such was the fame of The Western Brothers in later life, that
listeners sometimes wrote to enquire after their "old school".
Presumably, these inquisitive wireless enthusiasts wanted to
despatch their sons, nephews or young cousins to the same *alma
mater*. In fact Kenneth and George went to different schools. In
1937 they explained:

> We should like to satisfy the curiosity of so many of our correspondents as
> to the names of these schools, but we have been requested by the respective
> headmasters to hush the matter up. Apparently, they are afraid that hordes of
> souvenir hunters will descend upon the ancient buildings and start chipping
> lumps off the walls or disturbing bats in the belfry.

Possibly inspired by these earlier students, Kenneth, when merely eight years old, composed a magazine for private circulation among fellow pupils, a cheering mixture of doggerel, satire and caricature pertaining to the staff. These days, such a prank would be more likely to earn commendation for self-expression than any chastisement, but Kenneth was a student in the days before modern enlightenment replaced old-fashioned discipline. The headmaster was not amused by the magazine, and made it rather painful for Kenneth to sit down. Years later, now a radio and music hall star, Kenneth returned to the scene of his educational exploits. The headmaster, with noteworthy respect for a famous visitor, produced from the drawer of his desk a well-worn Class Attendance Book. Carefully opening the pages, the academic worthy pointed to a frequent entry, and commented: "Western, K.A. — Disorderly". Yet one of the masters at the school, hoping to channel Kenneth's literary energies into respectable journals, had suggested that he submit them to the humorous weeklies which abounded in the early years of this century. Alas, they were returned with those "Editor's Regrets" well known to writers in every generation. The practice at writing "funny verses" must have been valuable, given the subsequent demand for original material involved in radio broadcasting.

George, by contrast, confessed that he had been well-behaved at school, even securing a book prize for good conduct. This volume, *Fox's Book of Martyrs*, was collared by a sporting uncle, who possibly mistook it for *Fox's Book of Starters*. Despite his poor start as a balladeer, warbling "Alone on a raft", George soon began to enjoy success on the concert party circuit and, as the embryonic BBC "wireless" set out to both educate and entertain the nation, became an early broadcaster as pianist for "The Roosters Concert Party", an ensemble which had service origins from during the first World War. George had become so entangled whilst serving with The Queen's Westminster Regiment in Palestine. He was doing his best with a dilapidated piano in a YMCA canteen when a certain Sergeant Percy Merriman interrupted the service sing-song with a request that Western, G. "volunteer" for extra duties. These turned out to be pleasant enough.

The regimental concert party, known as "The Rooseters"*, had urgent need of a pianist, the regular accompanist having fallen ill, so George took on the job and, as the regular accompanist never returned to claim his sheet music, became a permanent member of the troupe. George thus secured an excellent entertainment training via the army, handling rôles in sketches, merry melodies and even female impersonations. On return to "Blighty" after the war, "The Roosters" decided to keep together rather than seek individual engagements — a policy sufficiently successful to secure a BBC audition. Broadcast engagements were hardly lucrative: in the early days the BBC fee worked out at a guinea (£1.05) per "Rooster". Percy Merriman who, as army sergeant, was responsible for George's involvement, was still going strong as a "Rooster" in the mid-1930s, as indeed were two other members of the original party.

Kenneth, some years younger than George, worked in the Army Press Bureau in London during the war. Later, he confided that "were it not for the Official Secrets Act, I could tell some strange stories of our spy system" — and this was long before *Spycatcher*, of course. Ironically, though he was eager to join the Forces on reaching call-up age in March 1918, the Army Press Bureau tried to discourage him. Kenneth was told by his chief that he was doing too important a job in London to be sent to France. Indeed, he had been given a permanent exemption. Kenneth, on the other hand, said that he did not want to be known as a "Cuthbert" (i.e. one who would not go). So, after a spot of regimental palaver, Kenneth was told he could report to the Royal Horse Artillery Depot at Woolwich for enlistment. The army, however, proved singularly uninterested in this solitary "civvy". Even when he insisted on joining the honoured regiment, the horse assigned to him seemed unimpressed by its new rider. Kenneth finally received his commission on November 7th, 1918. This news apparently proved the last straw to the enemy, and an armistice was negotiated soon afterwards. Alas Kenneth, though commissioned, had no officer's uniform, and military interest in his potential — already limited — now seemed to disappear altogether. Still, he had performed valuable

*Original spelling, later changed to "Roosters". The title was derived from the name of the unit's commanding officer, Colonel Roose, and in part inspired by that of the company officer, a Major Cockerell.

George at the controls of a biplane, with Kenneth, not entirely dressed for the part, ready to join him.

war service though, like so many of his generation, he was very modest about it.

Kenneth's partnership with George was the beginning of one of radio's most successful acts, The Western Brothers. He had become interested in comedy initially through fund-raising activities for a church football club, of which he was secretary. The fund-raising included a concert which, though otherwise appropriately supplied, lacked a comedian. Kenneth decided to accept the challenge and, in his studies of the art of comedy, saw some of the best acts in the business. Among the many excellent performers he observed from the gallery, an act known as "The Two Bobs" especially impressed him. These were "performers with piano", rather like The Western Brothers were to become, albeit with their own style. Whilst Kenneth had little trouble in producing stylish lyrics for such an act, he was a little short of musical back-up. At last, a kindly aunt suggested that Kenneth seek advice from his successful cousin, George. Although that encounter — at George's apartment — began with what Kenneth later described as "arctic dignity", the atmosphere soon warmed up. Before long, George was seated at the piano, conjuring up a melody that might reinforce Kenneth's lyrics. The result was a first collaboration — *Nineteen Hundred Years Ago* — enthusiastically adopted by "The Roosters Concert Party".

"Good evening, cads, your better selves are with you once again!" was the
customary greeting from Kenneth while George tinkled away at the piano.

From the almost spontaneous decision to create a double act based on unflappability and a grand piano, The Western Brothers found an unerring way to "the Great British funny bone". Of course, the inter-war period abounded in short stories about "lounge lizards" and none too bright "toffs" of the kind marvellously described by P.G. Wodehouse. Sometimes described as "two pukka sons of Caddery" or "Britain's Chief Cads", The Western Brothers created a superb blend of wit, social comment and gentle self-mockery. Their act, it could be said, had more polish than the church pews shortly before a visit by the bishop. Another point worth noting is that their diction was excellent. They could be heard with pleasure, and without difficulty.

Like many other wireless stars, The Western Brothers were much in demand on the variety stage, and eventually resorted to flying to reach their engagements on time. They were occasionally photographed in aviation attire, with Kenneth doing a "line in leaning" against the fuselage. Among the reasons for this interest in aviation were the inevitable crises linked with the motor car. On one nasty occasion, the dapper duo had agreed to entertain at Sevenoaks in Kent between their two evening scheduled appearances at the London Palladium. The Sevenoaks audience was appropriately enthused with the public school spirit as expressed by Kenneth and George, and with time hardly in abundant supply, they began their return to the metropolis. Seabridge, the chauffeur, seemed inclined to dawdle, and was instructed to step on it. The car objected to this use of the accelerator pedal and, after a few gasps, ceased operation. Seabridge examined the engine and pronounced its expiry. By now, less than half an hour remained before the London Palladium pit orchestra would burst into its introductory chords. Showing exemplary old school initiative, Kenneth and George managed to stop one or two cars and requested lifts to the West End. One of the vehicles proved to be a police car, but the uniformed men within were apparently preoccupied with a call to another duty. In any case, the duo were devoid of their monocles, not to mention their aura of unflappability. Fortunately, a car occupied by two bright young fellows zoomed up. They were naval officers, returning to their unit after leave. Taking no chances, The Western Brothers produced their monocles and peered in a superior fashion at the nautical motorists. There was no doubt about their identity, and it was thus thanks to the Royal Navy that the London Palladium variety performance was rescued from catastrophe. But, as they say of all the best crises, it was a close run thing!

Another aspect of public school life sometimes intruded upon the tranquillity surrounding The Western Brothers — namely, practical jokes. Bud Flanagan and Chesney Allen had a flair for, if not an actual college diploma in, jolly japes. So it was that when The Western Brothers arrived at the London Palladium to star with Flanagan and Allen in *Life Begins At Oxford Circus*, they sauntered into the dressing room occupied by Bud and Ches to offer greetings. They had hardly spoken when a generous shower fell upon their sleek and well-brushed brows, via a rubber hose connected to a cold-water tap operated by Bud. But when Bud attempted to perform the trick a second time, he found to his cost that certain "adjustments" by anonymous fingers now diverted the water towards him. But, as The Western Brothers confirmed in the *Radio Pictorial* of January 29th 1937, Bud could be intensely philosophic at times. On one occasion he approached Kenneth and, in a very thoughtful manner, enquired: "Do you know that your face is remarkably like ... Wolverhampton?"

In the same press interview, there was reference to another practical joke performed by Charlie Clapham (of "Clapham and Dwyer" fame). One Sunday morning, Kenneth and George were considering Mother Nature and next week's bookings in the front garden, when a milk float trundled by. There was perhaps nothing eye-catching in this, until the milkman proved to be Charlie Dwyer. He appeared to be auditioning for a part in a forthcoming production of *Ben Hur*. However, the true, legally-constituted milkman rapidly ended the performance.

Charlie Clapham, a well known broadcaster despite a modest speech impediment, abounded in bright ideas, and was largely

Clapham and Dwyer, a great comedy double act who were billed as "A Spot of Bother".

responsible for The Western Brothers taking to the air. An initial flying demonstration was given at Croydon Airport, as proof that flying was a marvellous antidote to the effects of late-night parties. Although aviation was regarded as entirely business-like, i.e. to meet the demands of a crowded appearance schedule, it had its show-business possibilities. At a Scarborough Air Pageant in the 1930s, The Western Brothers were engaged to hunt a "tunny fish", a gas-filled balloon shaped like an aquatic mammoth, from two piloted aircraft. Kenneth did his best, but the stunt arranger had omitted to allow for wind resistance. When he fired his gun at the tunny fish, from the rear seat of a biplane flying at 100mph, there was almost a nasty accident, for the recoil might well have ruined the prospects of old age on the part of pilot or passenger. George had no greater success: his shotgun's load found its way into one of the wings of Kenneth's aircraft. Following an attempt to dive onto the tunny fish, the ghastly balloon gave up the ghost and ended up in a bramble bush. On the whole, the performance had not added the names of The Western Brothers to the flying record books! Yet their example of "Chief Cads Aloft" could have inspired some of the RAF slang of the Second World War, much of which had the spirit of the old school tie.

During the 1930s, The Western Brothers appeared on commercial radio, especially the Sunday evening *Rinso Music Hall* transmitted on Radio Luxembourg and Radio Normandy. Compèred by Edwin Styles and featuring some of the era's best known radio stars — Tommy Handley, Elsie Carlisle and Teddy Brown, for example — the programme was one of the most successful from the continental commercial stations. Saturday night's *Music Hall* on the BBC Home Service was the perfect outlet for The Western Brothers. In the dark days of the Second World War, they countered enemy propaganda with songs like *George Washington Goebbels*, and, like many other popular radio artistes, helped entertain the troops. Although they never lost their popularity, The Western Brothers will always be associated with the 1930s, the last decade of the truly impeccable performer. Their film appearances were brief, though they showed their utter unsuitability for practical tasks in *Soft Lights and Sweet Music*, made in 1936. Today, a similar act would perhaps seem out of place, Britain having less of the spirit of "give and take" these days. At their best, however, The Western Brothers had a remarkable rapport with their audiences, expressed best of all in their sign-off comment: "*Do* look after yourselves. There aren't many of us left, you know".

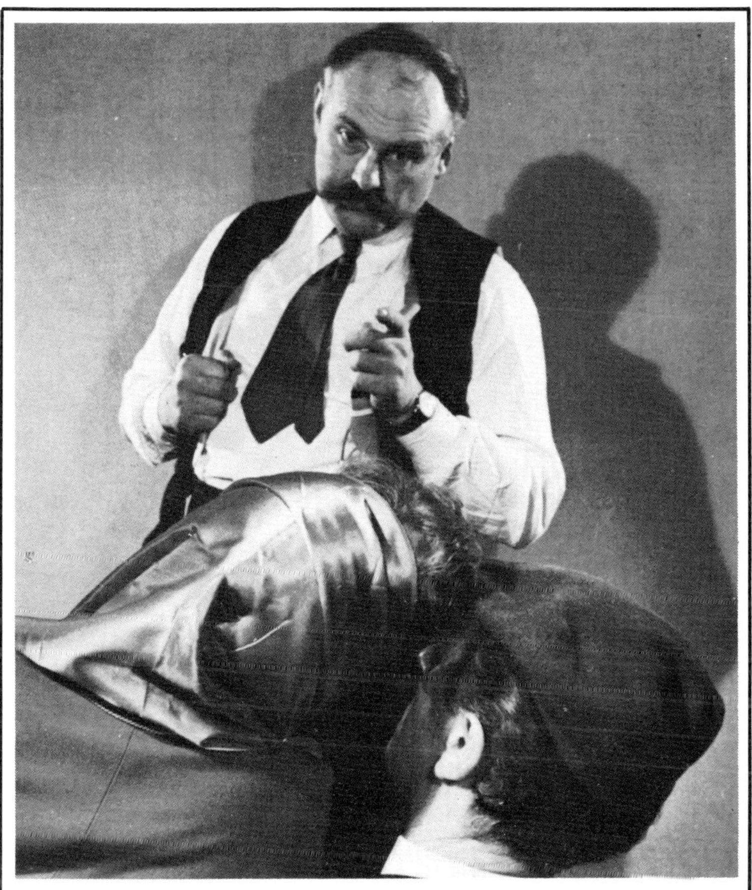

Take It From Here

This award-winning comedy series from the 1950s became the favourite programme of a great many listeners, not least for its satirical portrayal of a "Typical British Family", the Glums, played by Jimmy Edwards, June Whitfield and Dick Bentley (pictured above as Mr. Glum, Eth and Ron). The shows were written by Frank Muir and Denis Norden.

Chapter 10

The BBC's Penthouse: Arthur Askey and 'Band Waggon'

Although Arthur Askey was sometimes addressed as "you silly little man" by his companion and mentor, Richard "Stinker" Murdoch, his was one of the greatest talents on radio. Perhaps that is why he was known as "Big Hearted Arthur", a large red heart being stitched on the left breast of his "combs" — much mentioned years before thermal underwear became a mail-order bonanza. He was also an inventive man, possessing more inspired nonsense than ever the BBC allowed on the airwaves. Of all the great radio comics, Arthur Askey seemed best able to adapt to film-making, as, for example, the screen version of Arnold Ridley's *Ghost Train* showed. Invariably operating on tight budgets, British film makers somehow failed to make the best of his talents. However, he did his best, having the good fortune to star with Evelyn Dall, the singularly attractive vocalist, in *Calling Miss London*, in which Arthur starred as partner in a matrimonial agency. And why not? He was always "Big Hearted".

Band Waggon — the BBC comedy programme first broadcast in January 1938 — was also translated into film comedy, giving moviegoers the opportunity to see the stars of the show. The people in charge at the BBC were generally portrayed as stuffed shirts, with no time for "silly little men" wearing spectacles. In fact, the BBC seemed almost overwhelmed by the Spirit of Jollity in the last years of peace, and inspiration was certainly around when, in 1937, plans for a new kind of situation comedy programme were discussed. Involved in this enterprise were two

Richard Murdoch and Arthur Askey during a 1938 broadcast of Band Waggon.

men associated with some of the BBC's most popular programmes, Harry S. Pepper and Gordon Crier.

Harry S. Pepper was another broadcaster with an astonishing
fund of stories from his concert party days. His father, Will Pepper, ran a celebrated concert party at Clacton known as "The

White Coons". This title had no deliberate racial aspects, the minstrel shows of the time often wanting to suggest a genuine American musical tradition. Young Harry was soon incorporated in the family business, numbering seats, selling programmes and performing at the piano. Few pop stars are so fortunate as to enjoy such basic training! There were occasional shocks, as on the occasion that Pepper senior bought some old but serviceable sheets of tarpaulin to make a beach shelter in which to present the show. Unfortunately, the awesome word "Condemned" had been indelibly stencilled onto each tarpaulin, suggesting either a recent visit by an unkind critic, or even a drama by the Tod Slaughter Company. British summers being what they are, the shelter was last seen being blown towards the sea during a gale, with several stout-hearted local men doing their best to arrest its progress. During its all-too-modest life, the *ad hoc* marquee was used for an audition by two aspiring performers, young ladies neatly dressed in red skirts and yellow blouses, one of whom played the piano, and the other, the violin. These were Elsie and Doris Waters, at the time looking, as Pepper recalled, "as though they ought not to have been let out of school". As "Gert and Daisy" they were to have a distinguished radio and music hall career. In recent years, they have been the subjects of a biographical musical play.

As a BBC producer, Harry S. Pepper spent part of his summer catching concert party and pierrot performances around the coast, and looking for talent. His own broadcasting career had come through his membership of "The Co-Optimists", probably the most famous concert party of all. He later joined the staff of the BBC, writing music, producing programmes and occasionally performing. *Band Waggon* apart, his best-known programme was the *Kentucky Minstrels,* which was especially enjoyed for its close-harmony singing, a flow of 78 rpm records (HMV crimson label) being encouraged by the programme. Doris Arnold — of *These You Have Loved* fame — made a major contribution to the programme's musical quality. The *Kentucky Minstrels,* created in 1933, had been enjoyed for some five years prior to the "new sound" in comedy proposed at the BBC.

"The White Coons" Concert Party.

Situation comedy shows had proved their potential in America, though until the arrival of *Band Waggon* comedy on the BBC, it had consisted almost entirely of "turns". Music hall artistes arrived at the BBC for auditions and the Director of Vaudeville, or another relevant producer, would sit behind a screen to listen to, but not view, the performance. Some artistes took to the new medium at once, but others seemed lost without a live audience. Performers — booked up for months ahead on variety tours — could be singularly withering when any mere broadcasting upstart suggested changes to their act: "If it was good enough for the Royal Family, I don't see why it's not good enough for your contraption". When a weekly comic, *Radio Fun*, was published by The Amalgamated Press in the late 1930s, comic strips occasionally lampooned the self-important on both sides of the microphone.

The plot, such as it was, concerned two stout-hearted if slightly impoverished chaps, trying to get "on the wireless": Arthur and Stinker. In passing, one might note the excellent relationship presented to the listeners — far more sophisticated than the buffoon and straight-man duo usually adopted for variety or radio work. Arthur was perhaps innocent of the ways of the world, and needed his friend's advice in courting Nausea Bagwash, the cleaner's daughter (who was ever-absent, by the way). Stinker's advice that Arthur should announce that he had come to "press his suit" was so misunderstood that he declared he had come to "iron his shirt" — but radio comedy owed as much to zestful delivery as to originality. Arthur was no chump, however, and the pair were equal in status, though Stinker was, of course, the well-spoken "toff", in contrast to Arthur's more homely approach to life.

By some strange misdirection they found themselves in a flat on the top of Broadcasting House, a sort of abandoned penthouse with a splendid view over Langham Place. This, they thought, was a sort of waiting room, in which aspiring performers read *The Stage* and the *Radio Times* before being summoned to a producer's sanctum for the audition. As days, and presumably weeks, went by, Arthur and Stinker embarked on a necessary system of self-sufficiency, with Arthur's combs and nightshirt flapping cheerfully on a washing line strung between two radio transmission masts. Given the BBC's great interest in natural history programming, sometimes presented by staff members of London Zoo, the presence of a camel named Hector, and a goat named Lewis, hardly excited comment. Two pigeons, Basil and Lucy, perhaps helped the hopeful pair to keep in touch with their agent.

The title of the show was inspired by a Broadway musical, for Gordon Crier knew a great deal about the American theatrical and broadcasting scene. *Band Waggon* was later adapted as a highly successful MGM film starring another British "toff", the excellent Jack Buchanan. Originally, the new BBC programme was to have featured music more prominently than ultimately proved to be the case. The truth was that Arthur and Stinker stole the show, and the BBC began to receive fan mail addressed to "The Flat on Top of Broadcasting House". Another reason for the programme's success was the presence of the lugubrious rag-and-bone-man, Syd Walker, who presented a sort of mini-

This advertisement appeared in Radio Pictorial on 1st September, 1939. Two days later, of course, Great Britain was at war.

drama based on his experiences around the lesser streets of London. His sign-off catch-phrase, "What would you do, chums?", became part of the currency of everyday conversation. Stanley Holloway and Harry S. Pepper wrote the song performed by the rag-and-bone-man in what might be described as "Cockney bass". The song, "Any Rags, Bottles or Bones" was included in a 1980 LP retrospect of *Band Waggon, Happidrome and other great wireless Comedy Shows* (World Records SH388). Reginald Foort, the cinema and ballroom organist, was included in the programme.

Among the features associated with *Band Waggon*, "I Want to Be an Actor" would seem right for revival today. It was, in effect, a short epic presented by members of the studio audience, who applied for an audition before the programme's broadcast. Vernon Harris, a former rep and London stage actor, produced the feature, which in due course became a separate radio programme. *Band Waggon* proved to be lucky for this affable, bespectacled actor-writer. Following his work on *Band Waggon*, initially as a free-lance, the BBC offered him a full-time job as a radio producer.

At about this time, Arthur began to find a wider audience for the animal, bird and insect songs written by Kenneth Blain. "The Bee" ("Buzz if you like but don't sting me") was probably the best known and, with other Kenneth Blain songs performed by Arthur Askey, has been reissued on LP in recent years. Of course, the onlooker or television viewer also enjoyed Arthur's animated dance in imitation of the bee. Yet radio listeners lost little, if anything, of the performance, partly because Arthur's diction and delivery never fell from his self-imposed high standards. To hear Arthur read a passage from the Bible at a church service was to be aware of a tremendous potential for "serious" work. But comedy is serious, Arthur would have observed, and, flexing his muscles, might have enquired if we could see him in tights as *Hamlet* — or in his nightshirt, for that matter.

Band Waggon won well-earned plaudits for the BBC. Although the programme was broadcast for only 40 weeks on Wednesday evenings, and in radio history terms has since been eclipsed by Tommy Handley's *ITMA, Band Waggon* brought a new conception of radio's potential. Arthur and Stinker enjoyed further success on commercial radio in 1939, with the *Symington's Radio Show* broadcast on Radio Luxembourg on Sunday evenings at 9.15. This half-hour programme, recorded in London, also included Al Bowlly, probably the best-known crooner of the time, and "The Southern Airs", described as "The Crazy Kings of Rhythm". Publicity suggested that the programme was "The High Spot of The Week" but, whilst it had some noteworthy routines, it had no camels or goats.

In his private life Arthur Askey had burdens to bear, including the long illness of his wife. His own fight against ill health involved considerable surgery. A fellow artiste who saw him in hospital recalled that Arthur was too ill to speak, but none-the-less managed to give a thumbs-up sign. Such was the indomitable spirit of this talented and conscientious star of the wireless. There is no doubt that his concert party experience contributed to his success: Arthur was a master of the "aside", i.e. an apparently confidential comment to the listener or viewer. Such asides sometimes attained the status of catch-phrases, one example being: "Doesn't it make you want to spit!" There was also something very personal about his famous greeting, "Hello, Playmates!" It is well said that *Band Waggon* brought a "new intimate acquaintance" to radio. At the same time, it must have done wonders for the retail sale of woollen combinations.

Chapter 11

Tommy Handley: 'That Man' and Friends

The phrase "It's That Man Again", was reportedly composed by a newspaper sub-editor in reference to the latest outburst by Adolf Hitler, the German Chancellor. Abbreviated to "ITMA", the statement was subsequently linked with Tommy Handley, and to one of the most successful ever BBC radio programmes. Its bounty of catch-phrases, including such gems as "Can I do yer now, sir?" (Mrs. Mopp), and "Boss, boss, sumpin' terrible's happened!" (Sam Scram), was soon applied to countless domestic and work-place situations. Tommy Handley adroitly handled the challenge of bureaucratic bungling, administrative aberrations and diplomatic disasters, in capacities that included the Mayor of Foaming-at-the-Mouth, and the interpreter for a certain Frisby Dyke (Deryck Guyler), a gentleman from Merseyland eager to explore the dictionary at the Mayor's expense. His adenoidal "What's cacophony?", interjected into an otherwise cerebral conversation, offered proof of the native Briton's hunger for knowledge and, for that matter, home-made delights, brought by Mrs. Mopp the cleaning lady (Dorothy Summers). Her opening gambit, "I brought this for you, sir", invariably provoked the Chief to enquire as to the ingredients and immediately wishing he had not asked.

The programme, written by Ted Kavanagh, might be described as a series of interruptions loosely linked by a sub-plot. Or, at least, there was a sub-plot before it was sabotaged by "Funf" the spy (Jack Train), who seemed to spend most of his time on the telephone. Among other interrupters were Sam Scram (Sydney Keith), a sort of Transatlantic walking dictionary

"Who's speaking?" "Dis is Funf, your favourite spy . . ." Tommy Handley, con-sidered by many people to be the greatest wireless comedian of them all.

inclined to attacks of intense agitation; Signor So-So (Dino Gal-
vani), a gallant from the Mediterranean overwhelmed by good
feelings and mispronunciation; a stern secretary named Miss

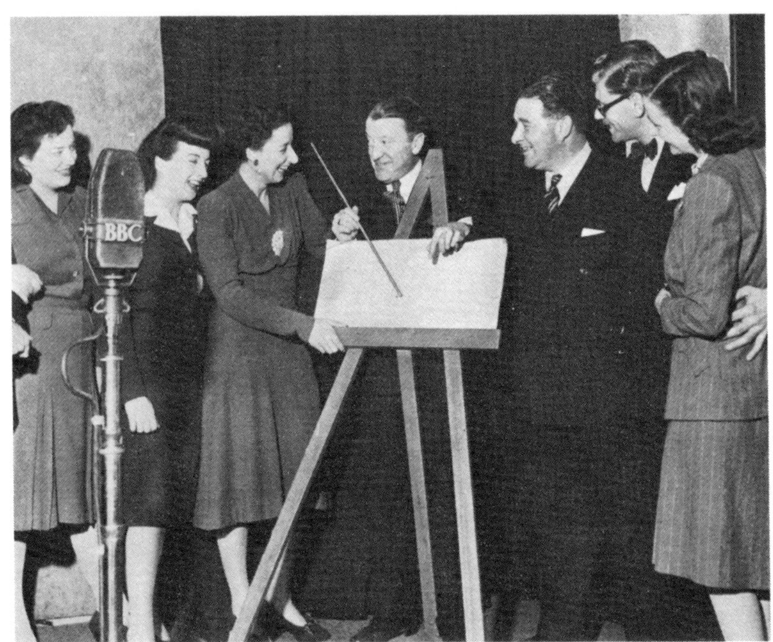

Hattie Jacques, Lind Joyce, Diana Morrison, Tommy Handley, Fred Yule, Deryck Guyler and Joan Harben.

Hotchkiss (Diana Morrison); and Ali Oop, a swarthy fellow eager to sell naughty picture postcards (Horace Percival). There were others, including the amiable orchestra conductor, Charles Shadwell, quizzed with astonishing perspicacity ("What's perspicacity?" asks Frisby Dyke) when announcing the musical interlude. A very detailed cast listing, covering the complete *ITMA* sequence, may be found in Denis Gifford's *The Golden Age of Radio* (Batsford), an encyclopaedic companion recommended to all wireless enthusiasts. The characters usually had something to do with Tommy's exploits as Minister at the Office of Twirps (an early wartime theme), as Squire of a very remote hamlet, or as Governor of Tomtopia (unknown to Sir Thomas More, writer of *Utopia*).

ITMA was broadcast on Thursday evenings between 8.30 and 9pm, and was repeated twice in the General Forces Programme, on Saturday evenings and Sunday lunch-times. Winston

Churchill and the Royal Family apart, *ITMA* was probably the greatest morale-builder of the Second World War. Following Tommy's death in 1949, a six-record set (at 78rpm) was released on Oriole Records as a show souvenir, and more recently an LP record on great radio comedy shows has included material by Tommy Handley. The show was also used as the basis for a British film, but it was hard to convey a primarily audio (listening) programme concept to the screen. Still, in all-too-large check cap and loud suit, Tommy on-screen showed, affably enough, that running a bureaucracy is a bit of a gamble for all concerned — something that the British had long suspected. Ted Kavanagh's genius in writing the show was in capturing recognisable elements of national character and then giving them additional colour. After all, nonsense is only normality writ large and *ITMA* was best described as "inspired nonsense".

The programme was born in the months immediately prior to the beginning of the Second World War, and was not initially regarded as a morale-booster — at least, not unless it was by the BBC directors, alarmed at the disappearance of audiences to lighter wireless fare on Radio Luxembourg and the other commercial stations. From the mid-1930s, the august and impeccable BBC had been criticised in the press for lacking theatrical expertise, and for expecting writers to work for only very nominal sums. Though the BBC at times seemed to be above criticism, there seems little doubt that a new spirit wafted along the corridors of Portland Place in 1938, aiding the development of excellent light entertainment. Thus, the creators of *ITMA* were given virtually free rein for their ideas, and, whilst being entirely original, they were almost certainly inspired by the fast-moving "zany" comedy shows heard on American radio, which, of course, received sponsorship. One might well debate whether or not the native American would have understood the *ITMA* vocabulary ("My mother had one of them and it stood on the mantelpiece," observes Frisby Dyke), but the programme style would have been familiar enough to them. *ITMA* seemed at times almost an exercise in tongue-twisting, especially as Sam Scram accelerated his explanation of the latest doom to befall the human race. In other respects, it provided a cheering interpretation of the anarchy which seemed to be overtaking humanity in the late 1930s. Whilst not specifying the shape of the golden future, the programme included reference to Tomtopia, an idyllic paradise where no vacuum cleaner salesmen called, and where graffiti was easily removed from the palm trees.

Tommy Handley recalled, in his biographical *Handley's Pages* (published in the late 1930s), that his first broadcasting engagement had all the effervescence of a day in the condemned cell. One morning in 1925, he strolled into the Savoy Hill studios of the old British Broadcasting Company, armed with a piece of sheet music and a surfeit of enthusiasm. He was an accomplished singer of light ballads, and a youthful Handley may be found lounging about on sheet music published just after the First World War. Tommy's voice might be described as "*basso profondo* verging on the ridiculous". From boyhood he had been able to sing in low registers, and was known (so he said) as "the lowest boy in Liverpool". He soon discovered the merriment to be exploited in quasi-solemn recitations of earnest monologues, when dropping from normal pitch to dark brown. Indeed, his vocal characteristics were amazing: he could imitate old gramophones, birds, animals, military goings-on, and much more. A bonus for his future career as an entertainer lay in his interest in sounds. Though he found his first encounter with the microphone about as cheering as Mrs. Mopp's cold waffles, he was in fact a "natural" for radio.

The producer welcoming Tommy Handley to the Savoy Hill precincts was a certain James Lester. As a departing suggestion to the aspiring broadcaster, Lester suggested that when Tommy Handley had finished his song, he might say "something funny". Later, Tommy realised that the request was made so that the studio engineers and the producer could secure a test of his *speaking* voice, i.e. as distinct from any register, scale or harmonic key signature used for the song. At the time, though, Tommy thought that his abilities as a comic were being scrutinised. There was an element of trauma in all this, Tommy later recalling that he stood in front of the microphone "literally gibbering

"Water, Sir?" "I never touch it!" Jack Train and Tommy Handley.

with terror". But after his blank mind had recovered from the attack, he burst into that ancient verse about days in each month. Even this, alas, was not entirely complete. However, the audition was a great success, and soon Tommy was involved in radio work. He became a member of the Radio Radiance Concert Party, and soon created his own radio revue programmes. In the early days of radio, good ideas could be quickly translated into programmes before the initial enthusiasm had worn off. Perhaps this helps account for the clear jollity radiated by the wireless, in a golden age of broadcast humour.

Tommy Handley showed remarkable stamina in handling a work-load that included provincial broadcasting tours, stage work, recording, and radio "specials" like pantomimes. He compèred the Royal Command Performance at Victoria Palace in 1927, having presented his legendary comedy sketch *The Disorderly Room* at the 1924 event. This was inspired by some of Tommy's Service experiences in the First World War and, as they say, struck a chord with the theatrical and radio-listening public. In those pre-recording days, almost all radio programming had to be "live", thus creating a heavy work-load for

Tommy Handley and Dorothy Summers in the "Victory" ITMA, May 1945.

artistes. It was impossible to record two or three programmes straight-off, as it were, and keep them "in the can" for eventual transmission. The Radio Radiance Concert Party at Savoy Hill, of which Tommy was a member, sometimes had to gather at the studio three or four times in a single week. Such devotion to honest toil brings its own reward, and it was at Savoy Hill that Tommy met the future Mrs. Handley, Jean Allistone. A talented actress, Jean Allistone had launched her stage career at the age of 11 (with Sir Herbert Tree), and had later worked for a number of companies, including Fred Karno. She was also a very acceptable principal girl in pantomime, and had great promise for the new medium of radio.

The marriage, which took place in 1929, had a brief honeymoon of two days secured between engagements, and the newly-minted Mr. and Mrs. Handley imagined that the ceremony had been kept virtually secret. Tommy explained the reason for this confidentiality was that he was "an old-fashioned fellow". On their journey back to London from the unspecified honeymoon retreat, they caught sight of a newspaper poster. It read: "Radio Romance", and as Tommy entered the BBC studio for that evening's variety programme, Jack Payne's Band burst into "The Wedding March" from *Lohengrin*. ("Wasn't that how you used to sing, Tommy?" enquired Frisby Dyke. "You used to sing *low an' grin!*").

In many respects a modest man, yet possessing something akin to genius for comedy, Tommy Handley had high regard for his audiences. Ponderous as it may perhaps sound in our "enlightened" times, he had a sense of responsibility towards those who came to see him on stage, or who tuned in to the radio. His attitude to his work was a great help to him when *ITMA* was proposed in 1939. Exciting as the prospect was, it involved a great deal of hard work, plus an element of creativity quite innovative in the field of British broadcasting. Tommy, like that other lively Liverpudlian, Arthur Askey, enjoyed the company of talent, regarding other performers as co-workers rather than competitors.

Not the least reason for *ITMA*'s success was the quality of its casting, some members of which later enjoyed distinguished careers in television, including Hattie Jacques, for example. Appearing with Eric Sykes in a brother-and-sister television situation comedy series, *Eric and I* (which also starred Deryck Guyler), Hattie had been a late-comer to *ITMA* (1947), but her sweet-voiced portrayal of Sophie Tuckshop was superb. Francis Worsley was responsible for the show's production, which must have been a labour of Hercules, who — to save enquiry from Frisby Dyke — was a gentleman who had a morbid fear of losing his luggage at the airport. Hence the phrase, "the seven labels of Hercules".

When Tommy Handley died in January 1949, more than 300 programmes had been made. Great crowds lined the streets at his funeral in Liverpool and, in retrospect, one could recall a sign-off song written for the show, *Tom Marches On*. He remains a gallant and glowing example for any humorist, in any medium. Although especially remembered for his work in radio, Tommy Handley had great affection for live theatre and the music hall, still flourishing, albeit past its peak, in the 1930s. His show,

Hello, Folks, did well — but as he had worked with Tom Walls and Leslie Henson after his "demob", Tommy Handley would have enjoyed the benefit of working with the best! In 1934, Tommy Handley and Ronald Frankau formed a duo known as "Murgatroyd and Winterbottom", an act sometimes described as "two minds with not a single thought". Tommy was the "Winterbottom" end of the partnership, and an initial press misspelling of the name as "Winterbotham" brought a letter of complaint from a real-life member of the noble British family of Winterbothams. However, the Winterbottoms remained entirely unmoved.

Ronald Frankau — brother of the novelist, Gilbert — was a popular stage, cabaret and radio performer, an immaculately dressed and suave deliverer of songs satirical and sometimes melodious, too. His "upper-class act" was accurately observed, for Ronald Frankau had been educated at Eton in the early years of the century. Apparently stage-struck, he studied at the Guildhall School of Music, whilst working at a family business office in London. When only in his late teens, shortly before the outbreak of the First World War, he travelled to Canada to exercise agricultural and journalistic skills. Later — after military service — Ronald Frankau spent time in India, touring and producing drama before his return to London. Ronald might well have followed his brother, Gilbert, into literary life, for he showed noteworthy prowess in short-story writing. Indeed, a directory of the 1930s suggests that he was sometimes mistaken for A.J. Alan, best-known of all radio story-tellers. (The directory adds that Ronald Frankau "wishes he was" A.J. Alan).

His entry to radio came via concert party work. Ronald Frankau's own company, "The Cabaret Kittens", earned a high reputation, so it was hardly surprising that he was invited to undertake auditions for the new world of radio. Soon he was broadcasting in *Children's Hour* as well as in "vaudeville", as the BBC described variety in the early days of the wireless. Radio might well have been devised for Ronald Frankau; his intimate style suited the medium. Indeed, he preferred to work without the presence of a studio audience.

Tommy pictured on his last visit to Blackpool, shortly before his death.

The double act was in the best tradition of well-bred, if not positively aristocratic, partnerships in radio and music hall. An exchange of quips, comments and gags included double meanings, up-dated chestnuts and, just occasionally, comments on current affairs. Sometimes, in preparing for a broadcast, Messrs. Frankau and Handley embarked upon an exchange of utter nonsense. Of one telephone conversation Tommy Handley remarked, "no eavesdropper would have been able to gather we were merely making an appointment for 10.30 next morning. He would have taken it for granted that we were insane."

Handley's Pages, the 1930s' autobiography, includes a tribute to Ronald Frankau's speed of response and delivery. Although Ronald Frankau's character and charm was typically English, Tommy Handley considered that "in a generation of comedians who are distinguished by the speed of their methods, he probably wastes less time than anyone I have ever heard". He had, no doubt, done some shrewd listening and learning during his stay on the other side of the Atlantic, since this impeccable pace had some affinity to American quick-fire comedy. Certainly, Tommy Handley regarded him as one of his closest friends, charming, talented and conscientious. The partnership undoubtedly extended Tommy Handley's range of experience, though one wonders how he found the time to do it. Ironically, some of Ronald Frankau's best songs, all written by himself, were considered too naughty for broadcasting, though they were available on 78rpm records.

If *ITMA* was the classic family comedy, Murgatroyd and Winterbottom showed what *might* be available when the children were safely tucked in bed. It was an act by two masters of the broadcasting art.

Chapter 12

Cinema Organists and Other Heroes: Sandy Macpherson with Friends

The BBC was so enthusiastic about cinema organs that it was rumoured Broadcasting House itself rose in time to the Wurlitzer. A favourite spot for theatre organists was the half-hour between 10 and 10.30am when, incidentally, the non-stop *Music While You Work* stimulated workers at home or factory. Happily, the BBC continues to encourage the many cinema and theatre organ enthusiasts, though most of the super-cinemas of the 1930s have long since been replaced by super-markets and office-blocks.

Best-known of the organist-broadcasters were "The Two Reginalds" (Foort and Dixon), and Sandy Macpherson. Long associated with the Tower Ballroom in Blackpool, Reginald Dixon had commenced his career as a cinema pianist, his auditorium, in an industrial village, being little more than a fair-to-middling hall. This modest background hardly impressed potential employers, even though Reginald Dixon's academic qualifications were excellent (he was an ARCM). Eventually, opportunity came for this Sheffield lad, though without much advance notice. One day, in 1926, he was asked to take over at a cinema organ in the unexpected absence of the normally-engaged musician. The option was of an urgent nature, but all those years of practice proved their value as, ultimately, they invariably do. Reginald Dixon, then in his early twenties, became organist at one of the new generation of Birmingham cinemas developing with the advent of "the talkies". His career

Sandy Macpherson, who during the first four weeks of the Second World War made 50 broadcasts.

was one of continuing progress and popularity, radio and recordings being of great importance. A 1930s' directory states that he found "a lot of romance in broadcasting". He certainly received many letters from appreciative listeners, including many involved in music studies. Although highly regarded for his performances of popular, dance and light classical music, Reginald Foort could have established a career in the classical repertoire. Among his own favourite composers were Bach and Schumann.

Reginald Foort — born in Daventry, home of the BBC's famous long-wave station — was also keenly interested in classical works. He studied the organ at Rugby, later going on to the Royal College of Music. When only a teenager, he was organist and choir-master at St. Mary's in Bryanston Square, London. Reginald Foort became increasingly involved with cinema organs following his demobilisation from the Royal Navy in 1919. A somewhat itinerant existence may have had its occasional problems, but travelling to musical engagements brought its own benefits, certainly by way of becoming well acquainted

with instruments and audiences. He played Edinburgh's first Wurlitzer organ (men have earned statues for less), and was soon broadcasting from cinemas. Indeed, the BBC paid him the rare compliment of following his career for broadcasting engagements. Although his first *organ* broadcast was made in 1926, Reginald Foort had been "on the air" earlier, as a pianist. He was certainly one of radio's first piano performers, the broadcast coming from Marconi House, London.

Reginald Foort might be described as the indefatigable organist. When he was "stationed" at the Paramount Theatre in New York, he performed six times a day, seven days a week, on a 10-week engagement. The theatre opened at 10am and closed at 2am the following morning. Included in Reginald Foort's repertoire during that engagement was Liszt's "Second Hungarian Rhapsody". ("Playing that 42 times a week was a bit of a strain", he observed).

A much-travelled organist, Reginald Foort was also something of an innovator during the 1930s, developing the slide-show technique for cinema work. After planning his music programme, Reginald Foort commissioned slides with appropriate illustration, pattern or effect, to link with the music. With a heavy schedule of programmes from the BBC, Foort commented that he had "great fun" with the BBC's theatre organ, "thinking out new combinations of stops, new selections and new methods of presentation". Listeners wrote in with suggestions on repertoire and arrangements, these being readily considered. One suggested an interlude of music with an animal theme, and mentioned some six melodies in the standard repertoire. Reginald Foort liked the idea, looked through his own music library of around 5,000 pieces, and finally produced a short list of animal subjects. From these, 18 pieces were developed as a grand "Animal Medley" — complete with dog fight.

Both Reginalds were popular broadcasters. Sandy Macpherson, however, had a rapport with listeners that is rarely achieved, and which in one sense moved him from one of London's super-cinemas to *Chapel in the Valley*. His warm Canadian voice was ideally suited to broadcasting, identifying him as a sympathetic, receptive personality. Ironically, Sandy Macpherson did not plan a career in music, still less in radio. Rather, he planned to become an accountant, perhaps following in his father's footsteps. Macpherson senior was a banker and Sandy's grandparents had been Scots who had emigrated to Canada years before he was born (they lived in Paris, Ontario). A juvenile interest in the organ had been prompted by young Sandy's attendance at a recital by an organist named Gatty Sellars. Sandy, then 12 years old, finally persuaded his father to arrange lessons. Whilst Sandy's promise in this direction became evident, he continued to pursue his career plan, as an accountant. Occasionally, he played the organ at a local church, hardly anticipating that he would one day become host and musician for a radio *Chapel in the Valley.*

Sandy served in the Canadian Armed Forces during the First World War, and although we know little about this period of his life, some stress may have affected his health, for he became seriously ill on returning to his accounting work. Physicians advised him to take a rest from all those figures, so, on a "temporary" basis, Sandy began to "fill-in" as pianist for a cinema orchestra in Hamilton, Ontario. Large cinemas had their own orchestras in the decade prior to recorded sound-tracks (i.e. the "talkies"), and the advent of sound films was to create massive unemployment among musicians on both sides of the Atlantic. One epochal day, the Hamilton cinema-owner called Sandy into his office, and asked how he felt about playing the Wurlitzer organ. He

Reginald Dixon, for many years the organist at the Tower Ballroom, Blackpool, and host, during the 1930s, of a regular request programme.

explained that the Wurlitzer's organist had fallen ill; maybe, he suggested, Sandy could "hold the fort" until the organist returned. In the event, the temporary arrangement continued to everybody's satisfaction until, in 1923, Sandy went to the United States to work for Metro-Goldwyn-Mayer.

Working for MGM was, to say the least, quite a challenge for the young accountant turned musician. His schedule included performances at handsome new super-cinemas, or playing accompaniment to major "silent movies". Among fellow organists met in America, Harold Ramsay was a temporary competitor when he and Sandy were performing at cinemas just across the street from each other.

Harold Ramsay, born in Great Yarmouth in 1900, was another fine musician and, like Sandy Macpherson, reached the USA, and later England, from Canada. He had left England

Another photograph of Harold Ramsay, which appeared in Radio Pictorial *on St. George's Day, 1937. He was due to be featured in the "Kings of the Cinema Organ" series on Radio Lyons.*

with his parents when a child, and whilst a choir-boy in Alberta studied piano and organ with Dr. Hodgson, who had come to Canada from Sheffield — Reginald Dixon's home town. Taking a degree in Music at the McGill University, Montreal, Harold Ramsay was involved in teaching and for some years, (1913-1922), was a church organist. This may perhaps seem a rather academic background for a cinema organist, but Harold Ramsay opted for this career, becoming resident organist at the Rivoli Theatre, New York, and, in the early 1930s, musical director of the Bernstein Circuit, which included some of Britain's most impressive super-cinemas. In particular, Ramsay frequently broadcast from the Granada, Tooting.

Metro-Goldwyn-Mayer assigned their star organist to a new super-cinema in Leicester Square, London — the launching pad, as it were, for MGM films in Britain. The original plan was

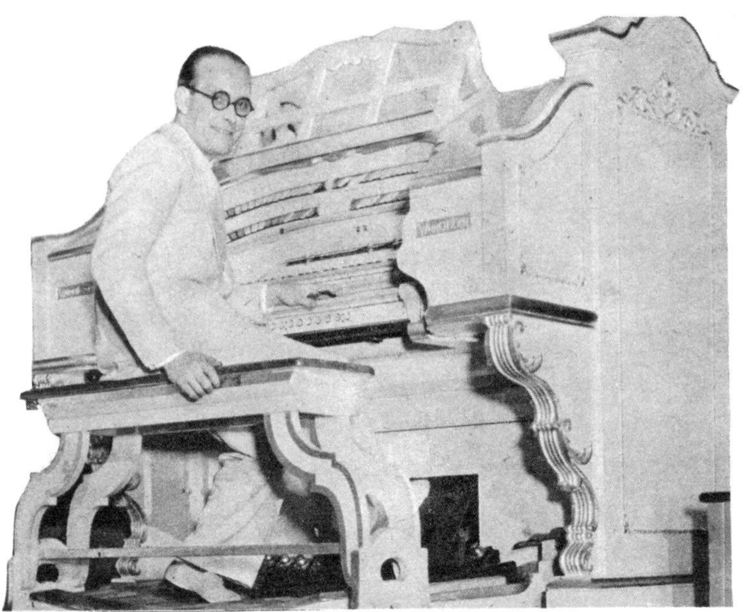

Another popular "organist of the airwaves" was Horace Finch.

for Sandy's stay to last for six months, before returning to the USA. In the event, the move proved permanent. Sandy's co-organist at the Empire was Reginald Foort, and, as they had to play the accompaniment for silent films, the work was exacting. Of course, the Empire, Leicester Square, was (and is) one of Britain's best cinemas, and in due course — after the advent of "the talkies" — Sandy was able to devote more time to his solo arrangements of familiar songs, which so delighted cinema-goers and listeners. These arrangements became the musical hall-mark of his work, and helped prove the possibilities of the cinema organ beyond special effects and cheerful tunes — the alleged limitations suggested by musical "perfectionists".

Yet Sandy Macpherson was almost a late-comer to the wireless, making his first broadcast in 1936. Nervous as he confessed himself to be on that occasion, he soon recognised the advantages of performing in an empty auditorium, and to a microphone rather than to an audience inclined to cough, chatter or wander up the aisle towards kiosk or toilet. To get the best from his performances, one had to *listen:* Sandy Macpherson was a true recitalist, not a mere provider of background music. He was, indeed, almost unique in his profession in talking about his solo arrangements, adding explanation links to his programme. His voice eventually became one of the best-known on radio. Radio Toulouse, the commercial radio company, invited him to present a Sunday evening programme, recorded at the Empire. These "melodies that linger" were woven into an arrangement aptly described as "a musical essay".

Sandy Macpherson had many friends, and it was well said that a "real brotherhood" existed among the cinema organists who, for example, gave assistance on arrangements, or substituted for performances during emergencies. Among his closest friends, Quentin Maclean remains especially worth recalling. To Maclean fell the honour of giving Britain's first cinema organ concert, and his weekly broadcasts from the Trocadero at the Elephant and Castle, London, were among the wireless highlights of the 1930s.

The Trocadero boasted Europe's largest Wurlitzer, though Maclean first secured his national reputation at the Shepherd's Bush Pavilion in the 1920s. Of all the great cinema organists, his introduction to this field was probably the most unusual. Born in London in 1896, he had begun organ studies when only eight years old, and was at the Leipzig Conservatoire by his early teens. His initial appearance as an organist at Bach's church in Leipzig was at the age of 15, and by the time he was 18 he was soloist at the Bach Festival. In a distinguished (pre-Wurlitzer) musical career, his labours included employment as Assistant Organist at Westminster Cathedral.

Like so many of his generation, the First World War considerably interrupted his career, yet, in a strange way, took him into the world of the super-cinema. A lecture-film based on General Allenby's campaign in the Near East during 1917-18, *With Allenby in Palestine*, was being shown in cinemas and public halls to large audiences. Quentin Maclean was recruited to provide musical accompaniment which, in terms of tempo and all round effect, had to match the action on screen. It was this experience that demonstrated to the young ex-serviceman the extent to which the organ could be used to accompany the then silent films. Thus, General Allenby's mission had the unexpected effect of bringing a classical musician into the world of the Wurlitzer. Quentin Maclean had outstanding talent, and it was said that he regretted the decline of silent film accompaniment. At its best, it had represented a genuine art form.

Undoubtedly, the cinema or theatre organists of the 1930s and 1940s represented varied backgrounds, often including academic and classical experience. Many, and perhaps most, noted early encounters with the local church organ, or even more advanced ecclesiastical involvement. Sandy Macpherson was entirely at home with the radio series for which he is probably best remembered: *Chapel in the Valley*. In essence, the programme — introduced by Sandy Macpherson — captured the "musical run-through" for Sunday church services (a routine known, in varying forms, as well to choir members and church organists today as to those of the late 1940s, when the programme was first introduced). No casting credits were given, though the young lady soloist, Marian, was in real life a member of the Luton Girls Choir. The village postmaster, Mr. Drewett, was organist, and a local farmer, Mr. Edwards, the choir-master. Marian was the daughter of the latter. Apart from explanation for the choice of some hymns or solos — a christening or harvest festival, for example — and a comment or two on the congregation's hymn preferences, *Chapel in the Valley* was devoted to music. Perhaps it owed much to Sandy's homely approach: at any rate, the listener had no difficulty in believing that he, or she, was really overhearing, as it were, a real-life preparation for worship being held later in the day. The programme continued well into the 1950s, being transmitted from 10 to 10.30 on Sunday mornings.

Resident in Britain and only infrequently able to return to Canada on holiday with his wife (also Canadian), Sandy sometimes missed the winter sports of his earlier years. Holidays taken at Engleberg in Switzerland usually included some bobsleighing, however, which is probably about as far as one can get from a cinema organ. His interest in ice-hockey was shared by another MacPherson, also from Canada but no relation. Stewart MacPherson, born in Winnipeg in October 1908, began his broadcasting career with the BBC as sports commentator in the late 1930s, a time (he recalled) when John Snagge and his associates were helping to build the BBC "as the masons of ancient times constructed Solomon's Temple".* A promising career — not to mention the building-up of the BBC — was interrupted by the arrival of war, and Stewart MacPherson was soon back in Winnipeg, working in the construction industry, but certainly not building any radio stations. The BBC had not abandoned this well-built, bespectacled Canadian, however, and in 1941 he was crossing the Atlantic to rejoin the Corporation as a War Reporter.

Dedicated to his craft, Stewart MacPherson proved an adaptable and thoughtful worker in radio. With Wynford Vaughan Thomas he developed a series of "on the spot" broadcasts, *Meet John London*, designed to lift the spirits of ordinary people during the war. He was also an early presenter of *Down Your Way*, preceding the programme's long run with Richard Dimbleby and Franklin Engelmann and later, Brian Johnston. Stewart Mac-Pherson had a special regard for the native Londoner, observing that in the *Down Your Way* series, "the cockneys made the programme breathe the very spirit of old England".

Another stalwart in the BBC radio schedule, *Twenty Questions*, had been heard in its American original by Stewart Mac-Pherson whilst on holiday in Winnipeg. Maurice Winnick secured performing rights for a possible BBC edition and, in due time, *Twenty Questions* was launched, the original panel including Richard Dimbleby, Anona Winn and Jack Train, with Daphne Padel joining the team later. Its success was astonishing, with television and stage versions being produced. One of the few drawbacks, as far as the production team was concerned, came in the mail from especially literate listeners questioning definitions and descriptions of "objects". From the extent of the correspondence, one might say that "the three R's" were alive and well in Britain.

Gordon Crier — who had been involved in the launch of

**The Mike and I, Home and Van Thal, 1948*

Band Waggon, the 1938 programme with Arthur Askey — invited Stewart MacPherson for audition on another comedy programme. *Ignorance is Bliss* was based on an American radio programme, again one in which Maurice Winnick had secured appropriate British rights. Although the BBC at first hesitated to broadcast so robust a programme, it was finally attempted and, after some "growing pains", proved a success. Gladys

The winner of the "Voice of the Year" award in 1949, Stewart MacPherson. Many people will remember him as compère of the crackpot quiz, Ignorance is Bliss.

Hay, Harold Berens and Terry Thomas were included in the team which tackled awkward, rather than awesome, questions of the day.

In an often hectic broadcasting career, Stewart MacPherson proved himself to be a "live wire" but, among all his credits, there would have been special pride in his live coverage of air raids on London, for onward transmission to listeners in the USA and Canada. He worked with Wynford Vaughan Thomas and Raymond Glendenning on the assignments, perched on top of a high building in Oxford Street while the bombs fell on the city. In more than the matter of cinema organs, Britons had reason to be grateful to broadcasters from the New World.

Chapter 13

Tune in Tomorrow: Radio Serial Sensations

But for the arrival of the Second World War, Britons might well have become radio serial enthusiasts in the early 1940s. By the late 1930s, the commercial radio stations based in Luxembourg and Normandy had adapted some of America's most popular radio serials for British consumption. These mini-epics, delivered in 15-minute doses, were known as "soap operas" in the USA, as indeed they are now in Britain. A half-century ago, radio producers were not entirely convinced that listeners would want to tune in, "same time, each day". Neither for that matter were the advertisers, whose expenditure kept the commercial stations in business. British advertisers linked to parent American companies were among the first to launch radio serials, probably encouraged by Vice-Presidents in charge of Radio Promotions based in New York or Los Angeles. A 1938 effort, broadcast on Radio Luxembourg at 10.15am on Sunday mornings, was sponsored by "Instant Postum".

No. 7 Happiness Lane was clearly aimed at housewives, for it featured the comings and goings at a theatrical boarding house maintained by a Mrs. Mary Gibbons, former leading lady at the Gaiety Theatre and now married to Jim Gibbons, who had played in the pit orchestra. (He was presumably no relation to Carroll Gibbons, one of the most popular band-leaders and pianists of the time).

Jim could have achieved great things in the orchestral world, according to some 1938 publicity for the programme, but — like some former City executives in these high-pressure times — had decided to abandon rushing around in favour of the quiet life. However, there were musical evenings at the boarding house,

Jon Pertwee, long before he became Dr. Who *or* Worzel Gummidge. *As well as appearing in* Marmaduke Brown, *Jon Pertwee was a long-standing member of the* Merry-go-Round *team.*

helped by Jim's daughter, Gladys, and her fiancé, a saxophonist named Tom Warner. As counter-balance to the unflagging enthusiasm for the theatre, *No. 7 Happiness Lane* included a certain Spencer Doughty Holmes, a Micawber-like actor who had not secured employment "since Shakespeare was a boy". A pleasant programme, definitely "up-beat", its listeners were invited to think about "those people who spend their working lives in the shadows of the stars — they're in the bright lights yet nobody knows them ... they have ideas, ambitions, emotions, loves, hate and talent".

These "romantic and dramatic episodes" from the boarding house were first broadcast in June 1938. Notwithstanding the occasional unflattering, if hilarious, references to theatrical land-ladies made elsewhere by comedians from time to time, *No. 7 Happiness Lane* had the elements necessary for success — plenty of characters, a whiff of greasepaint, music and a modicum of advice, i.e. other than the commercial message that accom-panied the programme.

Further evidence of the Transatlantic origins of the radio serial came with *Marmaduke Brown*, possibly the first true serial to reach Britain, in November 1937. In some respects, Mar-maduke would be very much at home in present-day Britain, his wife, Matilda, earning the family income whilst her spouse made plans — never realised, alas — of becoming an entrepreneur. Though described as "the story of an average married couple in an average small town", the programme could hardly have cap-tured conventional domestic life, at least not as it was then enjoyed in Britain. Marmaduke was a man with inventions on his mind, though far from being Britain's answer to Thomas Alva Edison.

The programme was presumably based on the American NBC radio serial *Lorenzo Jones*, described as the story of a garage mechanic who devoted most of his time to inventing apparently useless gadgets.* In the American version — sponsored by Phil-lips Milk of Magnesia there, as *Marmaduke Brown* was in Europe — the wife was called Belle. To ensure that housewives rather than gadgeteers tuned in to the programme, the publicity emphasised Belle's devotion, and that struggle for security which produced smiles as well as tears. Incidentally, the Radio Luxembourg version's cast included a young actor destined to become a TV master of gadgetry, Jon Pertwee, one of the more impressive "time-lords" of the *Dr. Who* series. However, it seems hardly likely that Marmaduke Brown ever made a "Tardis", or at least, not one that stood up straight.

*A dramatic scene from an episode is shown in *Radio's Golden Years* by Vincent Terrance, a guide to American radio published in 1979.

Stella Dallas — a best selling novel by Olive Higgins Prouty and adapted for a Samuel Goldwyn film starring Barbara Stanwyck — arrived on Radio Luxembourg in 1939, after an impressive beginning on the American CBS network. This was certainly one of the most successful of all American radio serials, being broadcast from 1937 to 1956. American radio rarely offered the dramatic presentations taken for granted by BBC listeners, though Orson Welles's *Mercury Theatre of the Air* (CBS radio) produced competent adaptations of great classics. Indeed, one of these, an adaptation of H.G. Wells's *War of The Worlds* broadcast in 1938, produced something of a national panic. Thus radio serials, with at least a kindly nod towards great literature, could do remarkably well on American radio. *Stella Dallas* dealt with the themes of parental sacrifice, the generation gap and the more enduring "homely values" in a somewhat materialistic world. It was sponsored by California Syrup of Figs, but, like so much else in Western Europe, was overtaken by the dark events of 1939.

There were also other pre-war radio serials for adults (children, incidentally, had been enjoying juvenile serials on BBC radio for some time). A few Radio Luxembourg offerings were quasi-serials in which prominent stars assumed rôles, one example being George Formby as a private detective in a Sunday morning serial of the summer of 1938. But these were hardly *true* serials, building up a family or community of fictional characters, as in later years the BBC was to do so successfully with *Mrs. Dale's Diary* and *The Archers*.

Among several attempts to measure the audience for the late 1930s radio serials, a "special announcement" offering a "surprise" was included at the end of one of the commercial station's transmissions. The "surprise" was modest enough, a free handkerchief accompanied by the greetings of the programme. Novelty value no doubt enhanced the audience response rate which was, to say the least, considerable. Indeed, a further radio announcement had to be made within a few days of the offer, this requesting that listeners write in no more letters. The experiment showed the drawing power of the radio serials and, even more, the interest shown by the public when articles were

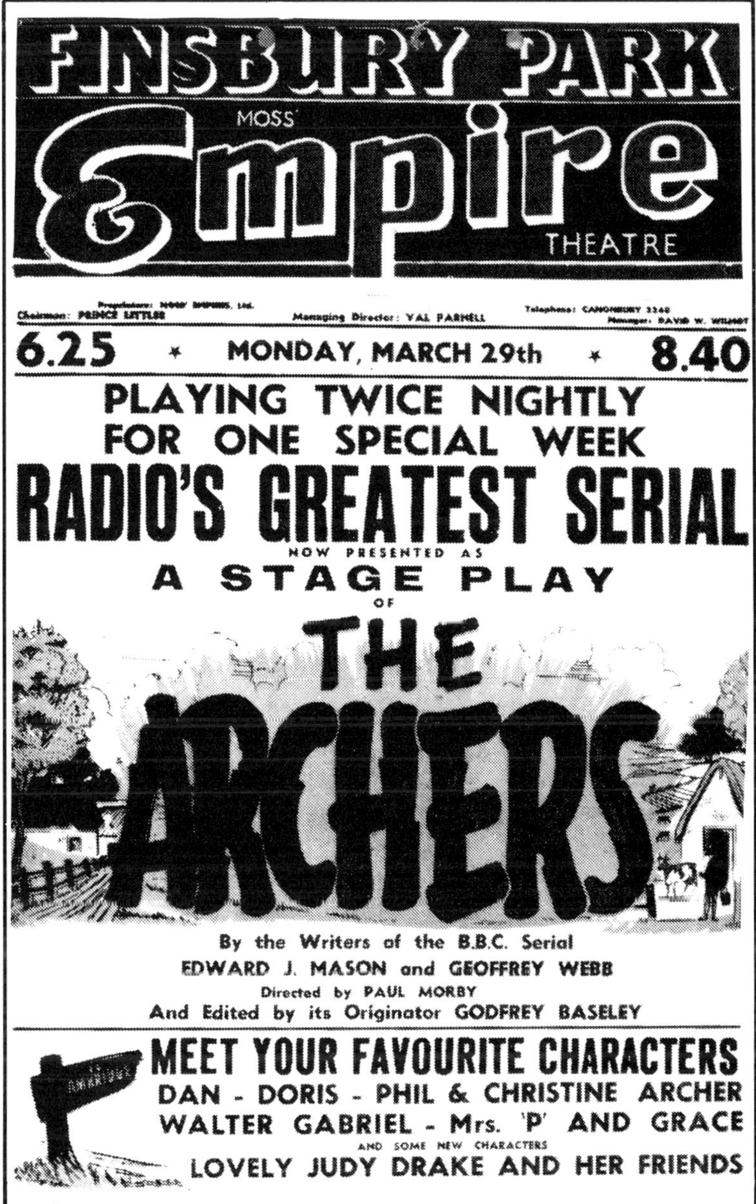

A poster advertising the stage version of the "everyday story of country folk".

127

The cast of The Robinson Family, a "Day-to-day history of an Ordinary Family" which was first broadcast on 30th July 1945. The series concluded on Christmas Eve, 1947.

offered free of charge. The estimated audience for the more popular housewife-orientated radio serials was approximately one million.

Although the BBC was embarking on a range of new programmes in the late 1930s, there was little interest in radio serials. Possibly the "soap opera image" brought sniffs of disapproval from higher management. In any case, there was no shortage of press comment about the possibilities of opening Britain to commercial broadcasting, so there was some sensitivity to the charge that the BBC was merely copying Radio Luxembourg or Radio Normandy.

At last, however, the BBC was converted to the cause of the radio serial — as a result of the Blitz. Given the testing and indeed threatening times in the land, the BBC decided that Overseas Service listeners should be assured that the Britons could "take it". Rather than add further straight news comment, the Corporation decided to adopt some of the characteristics of

128

the radio serial. The task of devising and writing the script for the *Front Line Family* was assigned to Alan Melville, well known at the time for the writing of revues and work at the Ambassadors Theatre. He also produced the programme which, having been first broadcast in April 1941, soon built up an impressive overseas audience. For reasons of wartime security, Alan Melville's untiring association with the programme was not mentioned. However, when he joined the Army the BBC reportedly brought in extra personnel to handle the workload, such was the success of this first ever BBC radio serial.

Front Line Family made its last broadcast in July 1945, after the surrender of Germany, and within a week or two of VJ-Day. The BBC, having long realised their inadvertent discovery of "radio gold", transformed the anonymous "Front Line Family" into *The Robinson Family* which, now broadcast on the BBC Light Programme, soon had an audience of five million. It ran until Christmas 1947 and, in a pioneering sense, touched upon the "north-south divide" issue, so often discussed today. Mr. Robinson was a North Countryman, though he had worked in London for some 30 years , and his wife a native of Scotland. Their three children were grown up and married. By late 20th-century standards, the programme might seem a little ponderous. However, it was well conceived, though it took *The Appleyards* on BBC television to create the idea of family life as entertainment. Mail, including occasional food packages, arrived for the Robinsons, care of the BBC, though the real breakthrough to a consistently large radio serial audience came with *Mrs. Dale's Diary*, the successor to *The Robinson Family*. Who could ever forget the harpist's introduction to the programme, first broadcast in January 1948, or the reflective comments of Dr. Dale's ever-earnest wife? The show continued for some 21 years until April 1969, its later star rôle taken by Jessie Matthews.

In its final years, *Mrs. Dale's Diary* was given a new impetus, the Dales even moving from their Middlesex suburb to a new town, full of the spirit of the new Elizabethan age. Radio comics and comedy shows loved to spoof the programme, using the soul-searching comment, "I'm worried about Jim" as allegedly uttered by the indefatigable diarist. Satire apart, *Mrs. Dale's Diary* was very popular with the (older) women's radio listening audience: in our health-conscious times, a similar vehicle, written for a changing social environment, could perhaps be useful in conveying aspects of personal health care. In the 1950s, social workers sometimes proposed that radio serials like *The Archers* could be especially effective as vehicles for advice on the use of credit — a timely comment.

Dick Barton was undoubtedly the most exciting radio serial devised by the BBC in the immediate post-war decade. Though British to the hilt — Dick Barton had been a commissioned officer in the Commandos — this hectic radio serial had echoes of American productions. Crime-fighters, spy-chasers and secret agents had abounded on the American airwaves for years, triggering a range of programme-linked souvenirs and ephemera much sought after by present-day collectors. In the early or mid-1930s, the idea of a daily radio serial, featuring blood-and-thunder situations, would have made BBC executives gasp into their mulligatawny soup. But in the bleak austerity decade of the later 1940s, the proposal was welcome. Given the fuel crisis of the time, and the harsh winter of 1946-47, anything likely to aid blood flow was welcomed. The daily dose of Dick Barton was provided at 6.45pm and preceded by the unmistakable music of "The Devil's Galop" by Charles Williams. A mixture of stiff upper lip, unmitigated villainy (about to bite the dust), astonishing perils and awesome sound effects, *Dick Barton — Special Agent* was sometimes described as a comic-strip of the air, this hardly impressing old-fashioned moralists and parents wanting their children to get on with their homework. What the programme lacked in intellectual stimulus, however, it certainly possessed in energy, and special effects. Three writers worked on the programme, which was a clear success from its introduction on Monday 7th October 1946. Each adventure was written for a four-week "start-to-finish" project, the best-known writer associated with the programme being Edward J. Mason.

The juvenile audience seemed to have their encyclopaedias at

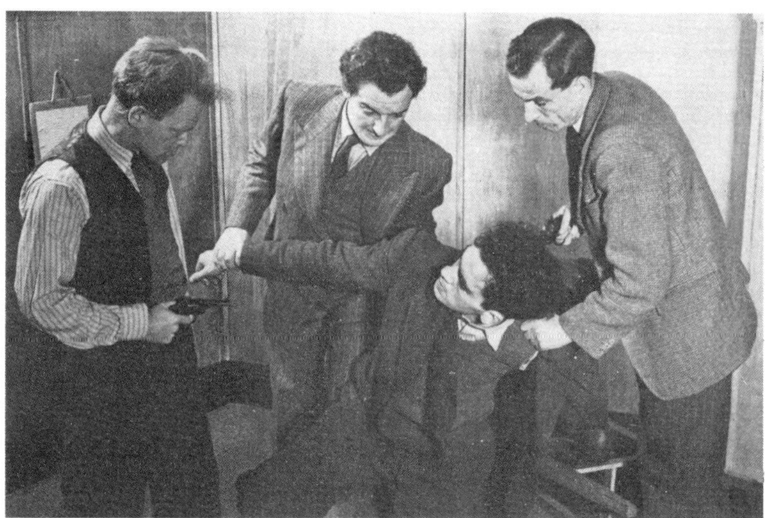

An exciting moment as Dick Barton, Snowey White and Jock Anderson over-power a villain — using minimum force, of course!

their elbows on tuning in. Any inadvertent departure from scientific fact of geography, chemistry, physics, etc, would bring mail from young fellows destined for academic distinction. In one episode, the gallant Dick Barton was left chained to an immovable post on a remote Mediterranean shore, facing death by drowning "as the tide came in". Among reproving mail soon received was explanation of the Mediterranean's characteristics, including the utter impossibility of anyone being submerged by a tide, since there were none. Suitcases full of paper money — an essential ingredient of spy thrillers in a pre-inflation era — also came to grief, as clever little chaps explained to the BBC that the quantity of banknotes mentioned in the programme could hardly be contained in any suitcase of dimensions yet used, or, for that matter, carried by an ordinary mortal. At times, one was reminded of Ronnie Waldman's "Deliberate Mistake" in the great days of *Puzzle Corner*. Did *Dick Barton*, too, leave an occasional red herring as a spur to mathematic measurements? That could have been a feather in the BBC's hat, when accused of mere frivolity.

The heroic trio in the programme, Dick Barton (Noel

Johnson), Jock (Alex McCrindle) and Snowey White (John Mann), worked hard to give authenticity to situations which at times seemed unlikely. Noel Johnson was a member of the BBC Drama Repertory Company for some three years before being offered the "Dick Barton" part. The programme continued — with breaks — until the end of March 1951, though a special stereo production was included in the BBC's 1972 Jubilee Celebrations. It is rumoured that the programme ended in time for the Festival of Britain, in order that Dick Barton could guard the Skylon on the South Bank site, this amazing structure being the target of several large men with snow on their boots, either determined to pick up a good souvenir, or mistaking the cigar-shaped wonder as a secret weapon.

The radio programme prompted a film (*Dick Barton Strikes Back*), an annual, and other spin-offs, but in those austere times the character was not commercially exploited to the extent that might have been possible, say, 20 years later. With praiseworthy commercial flair the BBC retained full original copyright to the character, yet must have been a little surprised at the range of criticism. There were allegations that British homes, once tranquil, were riven by argument as children insisted on listening to *Dick Barton* at the very moment their parents wanted to hear an organ recital or madrigals on the Third Programme. Among the more exaggerated criticisms were those suggesting that *Dick Barton* was projecting a political bias, i.e. towards Conservative values. The Labour Government, hard-pressed to meet the nation's reconstruction tasks, was perhaps too sensitive to media criticism, real or imagined. Press photography of the heroic trio in the BBC studios showed them wearing shirts, ties and conventional attire, with Dick Barton in a three-piece pin-striped suit — there was no bowler hat, though!

Controversy helped the programme, of course, and tall tales about real studio emergencies found their way into the press, one revealing that an actress had been unable to entirely satisfy the producer with a scream of horror. Then, whilst some equipment adjustment was being made, she produced a superb spine-chilling scream. Eminently satisfied, the producer went to offer

Rehearsals in progress for an episode of Paul Temple and the Curzon Case, *with Leslie Perrins, Duncan McIntyre, Marjorie Westbury and Kim Peacock.*

his congratulations, only to find the actress slumped to the floor. On being revived, she explained that a large rat had leaped from a ventilator intake onto her shoulder, this producing the required scream just before she fainted. One cannot help thinking that some bright spark involved in programme publicity concocted such yarns to retain press attention.

After *Dick Barton*, radio serials tended to be something of an anticlimax. There was a rare vigour and buoyancy in the programme. In contrast, the *Paul Temple* serials were suave, sophisticated and cerebral. This celebrated amateur detective first appeared on the Midland Region in 1938, so he was a native of Birmingham rather than Baker Street — even if a 1940s writer suggested that Paul Temple was more widely regarded than Sherlock Holmes.

From the first *Paul Temple* serial, the central character enjoyed public esteem, measured by fan mail and favourable reviews. Francis Durbridge, the writer, approached his work with meticulous care, and concentrated on no more than two serials a year, though within 10 years of Paul Temple's first appearance, some five novels had also been produced. The cost of success had a rather different outcome to that experienced by the *Dick Barton* team. Politicians and other gentlemen of moral distinction were less likely to criticise the *Paul Temple* serials than to offer their own real-life experiences as a basis for the next dramatic plot. As *Paul Temple*, in various guises, also did well on European radio services, the extent of these suggestions may be surmised. Martyn C. Webster, the radio producer, was among the most successful of all producers in the field of radio serials, developing a character into something approaching a radio legend, enigmas and all.

The *Paul Temple* serials, though developed by the BBC, had a link with Radio Luxembourg. When, in the late 1940s, a Paul Temple film was made, the main rôle was taken by John Bentley whose pre-war radio work included that at the Luxembourg studios. Publicity of the time indicated that it had taken the film-makers six months to find the right man for the rôle. Yet, even with successes like the *Dick Barton* and *Paul Temple* serials, the BBC was confronted by a fickle listening public. Who now remembers the radio serial that replaced *Dick Barton*? The spring 1948 launch of *Adventure Unlimited* was hopeful enough, but its heroes, Jackson and Sam Steed, hardly caught the headlines. *Riders of the Range*, introduced in the following year, had greater authenticity, its originator, Charles Chilton, giving a real-life flavour of the Old West. Western themes had long enjoyed large radio audiences in American radio, but *Riders of the Range* was described in the *Radio Times* as "a musical drama of the West" rather than as a serial. In one sense, the most exciting era of "radio serials" ended when Dick Barton struggled from a flooding cellar or blazing wreck for the last time.

Today, radio and TV serials are taken far more seriously, even solemnly, with the characters portrayed even being described as an "extended family" in relation to the viewer or listener — a patently ridiculous claim as there is no genuine interaction between real-life people and the entirely fictional characters. Perhaps the 1940s commentator had a point when he suggested that serials flourish in an age of monotony and boredom. There remains but one question: Did Dick Barton ever meet Stella Dallas?

Songs on the Wireless

The cover of this old song book, which recalls some great musical memories from the golden age of the wireless, is sure to start many people off humming the tunes and tapping their feet to the rhythms. During the 1930s almost every programme had its own instantly recognisable signature tune, and readers will be able to remember many other favourites.

135

Chapter 14

'The Kitchen Front': Food Advice from the Music Hall

The "wonderful wireless" came into its own as a public information medium during the Second World War, and especially in respect of nutrition. Food rationing ensured "fair shares" but certainly demanded flair and imagination on the part of housewives. Lord Woolton, Minister of Food, had extensive experience as a senior executive of Lewis's, the retailing organisation, and had been in charge of boot supplies for the Armed Forces during the First World War. An energetic, thoughtful and kindly man, Lord Woolton was a true social reformer, free from that self-assertiveness that sometimes passes for political maturity. He also proved himself possessed of natural talents in the use of radio for effective and cheerful nutrition education. In developing these gifts he was considerably helped by Howard Marshall, a well-known broadcaster assigned to the Ministry of Food. Together, they counselled and trained many home economists and nutritionists for *The Kitchen Front* and other short programmes providing food advice and recipes.

In his *Memoirs*, published by Cassell in 1959, Lord Woolton described his broadcasting task as "the simple, if one-sided, conversation of a visitor admitted to the home on the sufferance of a switch. It is no easy job, and worth all the time taken by long preparation and rehearsal to achieve simplicity." He added "The next thing I decided was that the public was either going to laugh or cry about food rationing, and that it was better for them that they should laugh — even if it was only a somewhat wry smile — than that they should contemplate too much on the misery of their position".

Armed with this sensible psychology, Lord Woolton consulted two experts in communication, Elsie and Doris Waters, whose "Gert and Daisy" music hall (and radio) act expertly captured the innate humour of "chars" (i.e. cleaning ladies) everywhere, though in their case expressed in a Cockney idiom. Once Lord Woolton had explained his concept of nutrition education delivered with a smile, his vis-

"CARE TO LISTEN TO THE KITCHEN FRONT?"

itors experimented with a few off-the-cuff Gert and Daisy exchanges. The Minister was delighted, and on their subsequent theatrical tours Elsie and Doris Waters planned food economy forums with the mayors and other officials of the towns and cities in which they were playing. There was an element of genius in Lord Woolton's idea, and in its expression by broadcasters with little previous experience in nutrition education.

Also involved in the programmes were the celebrated members of "The Buggins Family", created in the 1920s by Mabel Constanduros and Michael Hogan. Both were experts in Cockney character and dialect, and in her childhood Mabel Constanduros had accompanied her father, Stephen Tilling, on visits to his tenants in the Walworth Road area of London. Here, one suspects, young Mabel gathered the raw material for *The Buggins Family* — which first appeared in book form in the later 1920s. Indeed, she refers to later visits to the area in the preface to the book. With Michael Hogan, Mabel Constanduros outlined a family which had real-life models in the shape of two friends, Ag Peters and Bert Hodges. With her considerable drama training, including study at the Central School of Speech Training and Dramatic Art, Mabel soon proved to be a "natural" for the new medium of the wireless.

Like Mabel Constanduros, Michael Hogan was involved in acting and writing. A Londoner born in 1898, he had studied at RADA, and made his first stage appearance at the Savoy Theatre in 1914. After war service, and post-war experience with the Liverpool Repertory Theatre, he joined the BBC Repertory Theatre in 1925 as "leading juvenile", before concentrating on radio work from 1931.

At first the Buggins Family was entirely female, as Mabel Constanduros created all the voices. It therefore had a domestic background, in its way preparing for *The Kitchen Front* broadcasts. Michael Hogan's flair for the Cockney accent permitted expansion of the family to include a husband and son. Thus, the Buggins Family of Halcyon Row included Grandma, Mrs. Buggins (Edie), Father (Bert), Emma, Alfie and Baby. Other characters included Aunt Maria, friends, neighbours, Cousin Harold and callers; the programmes were in their way a model of that extended family life so much a feature of Cockney London in the years preceding the Second World War. Mrs. Buggins — bless her — was described as "a good-natured, much tried housewife".

Even apart from this drama preparation for work in nutrition education, Mabel Constanduros had considerable interest in "growing your own food" — a recurring theme of Ministry of Food broadcasts and leaflets. When, in 1931, she bought a cottage at West Burton, Pulborough, Sussex, Mabel Constanduros developed a garden that was abundant not only in flowers, but also in apples, currants, gooseberries, raspberries and other "home grown crops".

Michael Hogan's eventual departure to the USA to pursue a writing career, meant that Mabel developed *The Buggins Family* as a solo performance (John Rorke sometimes "appeared" as Father in radio transmissions), though she was involved in many other drama and writing commissions. By the late 1930s, Cow &

Gate Baby Food
was sponsoring *At
Home With the Bug-
gins Family* on
Radio Normandy,
one of the new com-
mercial stations giv-
ing so much com-
petition to the
BBC.

Programmes were
recorded on trans-
cription disc in Lon-
don, then flown to
Normandy from
Croydon Airport,
usually on a de
Havilland Rapide which also provided a shuttle to Radio

*"The Cookery subject is Tripe and how I
dish it up"*

Luxembourg. Grandma Buggins, with her deep Cockney voice
and expressive sniff, was understandably described as "a real old
corf drop", and continued to take the rôle of family critic when
the Buggins took up employment with the Ministry of Food.

The BBC's series of *Kitchen Front* programmes included
"straight talks" and discussions, but none were as popular as *The
Buggins Family*, where the conversation was always true to life,
and which included a useful recipe plus dietary information.
Years later, the contribution of these programmes to the healthy
diet of Britain, at a time of often severe food shortages, was
noted. So popular were the programmes that Mabel Constanduros was asked to visit women's groups in halls up and down
the country, as a sort of extension education initiative arising
from the programmes. Not that Mabel Constanduros thought of
herself as a skilled home economist, rather than an actress and
writer.

Lord Woolton seems to have been reluctant to leave the
Ministry of Food when, in October 1943, Winston Churchill, the
Prime Minister, informed him that he was to be appointed

The irascible and obstinate Grandma Buggins, created and played by Mabel Constanduros.

Minister of Reconstruction. This reluctance had much to do with Lord Woolton's intention to return to business once the war was won. But "Winnie" was adamant — that was that. In retrospect, we can see the great contribution made to national well-being by the programmes which Lord Woolton, Howard Marshall and their friends made. They remain something of a model for our own times, when nutrition remains an issue of vital importance, though in a different context to the 1940s.

Mabel Constanduros wrote some 100 radio plays and 40 one-act plays during her career. Among her film credits was that of the 1947 Ealing Studios production that brought "The Huggetts" into prominence, *Holiday Camp*, with Jack Warner, Kathleen Harrison, Petula Clark and Jimmy Hanley, all well known to radio listeners. She also collaborated, with Michael Hogan, on writing monologues for Stanley Holloway — what one might call a cheerfully lugubrious undertaking. Of all her work, though, none was more enduring than the invention of "the old corf drop", Grandma Buggins. When, during a radio programme, Grandma Buggins lost her false teeth, sympathetic listeners sent in replacement dentures, carefully wrapped in cotton wool and tissue paper. If any domestic argument occurred — as required by the script — listeners offered advice to the parties concerned, occasionally sympathising with Grandma Buggins that "people got no manners these days". She found her way — no doubt clad in thermal underwear — into many programmes, from *Monday Night at Seven* to *Children's Hour*. Reportedly in her eighties at the time of her early appearances in the 1920s, one might say Grandma Buggins enjoyed a ripe old age with the BBC 20 years later.

Mabel Constanduros died in 1957, and Halcyon Row — that traditional setting for the Cockney Buggins family — has probably been long-since demolished. The sound common sense from Grandma, though, has hardly been superseded by some of the flashy views around today.

Chapter 15

Jam Jars and Dahlias:
Broadcasting from Bristol

One of the nation's best-known vintage radio businesses is well-established in Bristol, an appropriate enough location given the city's pioneering work for the wireless. During the Second World War, some of the BBC's best-known programmes were broadcast from Bristol, though, heaven knows, the city was no stranger to enemy bombing. Colston Hall, a traditional home for temperance rallies and brass band concerts, became home for *Henry Hall's Guest Night* and other favourite programmes. A reporter told readers of a popular weekly of the period that Colston Hall looked "rather Victorian from the outside". One wonders what he would have made of Alexandra Palace, the original home of the BBC television service.

Surprisingly enough, given Bristol's present status in the broadcasting network, the early days of "the wireless" included no Bristol-based station. In 1925, the galaxy of local radio stations operating under the British Broadcasting Company included a main station at Cardiff (5WA), and a relay station at Swansea (5SX). Bristolians who had conjured up their sets from construction kits and sheer imagination thus had to pick up their

signal from Cardiff, or, if their sets were sufficiently powerful, from Birmingham. Bristolian celebrities wanting to utter their thoughts on air had to travel to Cardiff, just as in later years Welsh professors had to come to Bristol. You might say that the wonder of wireless did wonders for the Great Western Railway; it's surprising that Isambard Kingdom Brunel did not invent radio himself!

Listeners living close to the Bristol Channel often picked up their best signal from the Welsh transmitter. Even in the television era the Wenvoe transmitter, near Cardiff, offered a better signal than any other source to many Bristolians. As I discovered during my own years in radio/TV retailing in that historic city, any salesman worth his salt often had to explain "the mysteries of the ether", and maybe the benefits of listening to the Welsh, rather than the Bristol, news.

That kind of problem was all too familiar in the 1920s and 1930s. Many Welsh listeners could not receive the radio signal from Cardiff, but tuned in to Daventry with ease. Thus, among the other topics of discussion beloved by Bristolians, including temperance and the bus service, there was continuing interest in the elusive nature of the radio signal.

To encourage this discussion further, "Bristol Radio Weeks" were held. That of November 1928 included a dinner attended by local dignitaries, radio dealers and other optimists. Mr. E.R. Appleton — director of the Cardiff station — acted as chairman, and according to the *BBC Handbook* for 1929, "enthusiastic speeches were made by various members of the wireless trade in Bristol". During the 1930s, as studio facilities were developed on both sides of the Bristol Channel, Mr. Appleton had quite a job on his hands. As West Regional Chief, he had to balance requests for more Welsh language broadcasting with a growing demand for West regional interest programmes. He must have been a man with a marvellous sense of balance, and was himself a popular broadcaster. Included in the output was such light entertainment as the Sunshine Carnival from Weston-super-Mare. This event in 1928 raised over £1,500 for the local — and then new — hospital's X-ray department. Local talent opportunities were more abundant on the regional and local stations of the 1920s than is the case today.

Whilst the local advisory committee met regularly at Rotary House, Bristol, to consider programmes and progress, there must have been quite a few local "radicals" impatient at the pace of events. The Lord Mayor of Bristol acted as chairman of these matters, or, in his absence, the former Postmaster of Bristol, Mr. F.C. Luke. Some exasperated mail must have reached the headquarters of Sir John Reith and his successors, relating to the lack of a radio frequency specifically for the West Country. As the 1930 *BBC Yearbook* observed, you could find the same spirit of romance either side of the Bristol Channel, but tastes were different. All the same, the report of broadcasting in the West Country took less than a page in the report. Programmes originating in the West Country were transmitted from Cardiff, or fed into the national radio network.

The Clifton Arts Club seem to have enjoyed a handsome share of radio time, and among their repertoire offered a special programme devoted to Somerset life and music. The Bristol University Madrigal Singers performed their own style of music, whilst the Pump Room at Bath also welcomed the large and temperamental microphones, though the music therefrom was not as lusty as that featured in the *Sailors' Concerts*, broadcast, as the publicity put it, "from historic ships in the Bristol Docks", including the legendary *Flying Fox*. Ah!, if only Bristol had enjoyed the presence of Brunel's great iron ship in those wireless days — the *Great Britain* could have acted as a marvellous acoustic echo chamber for locally performed Gilbert and Sullivan. At least the two etheric fringes of the Bristol Channel were united by good tastes in music. One of the West Country's most popular broadcasters, Mr. Fred E. Weatherly (composer of a handsome array of ballads) often travelled to Cardiff to talk about his work. He died in September 1929, at a time when discussion of a new regional plan for broadcasting was well under way.

It was this new regional scheme, largely shaped by the remarkable Captain Peter Eckersley (Chief Engineer for the BBC), that helped Bristol get its own studio facilities, if not its

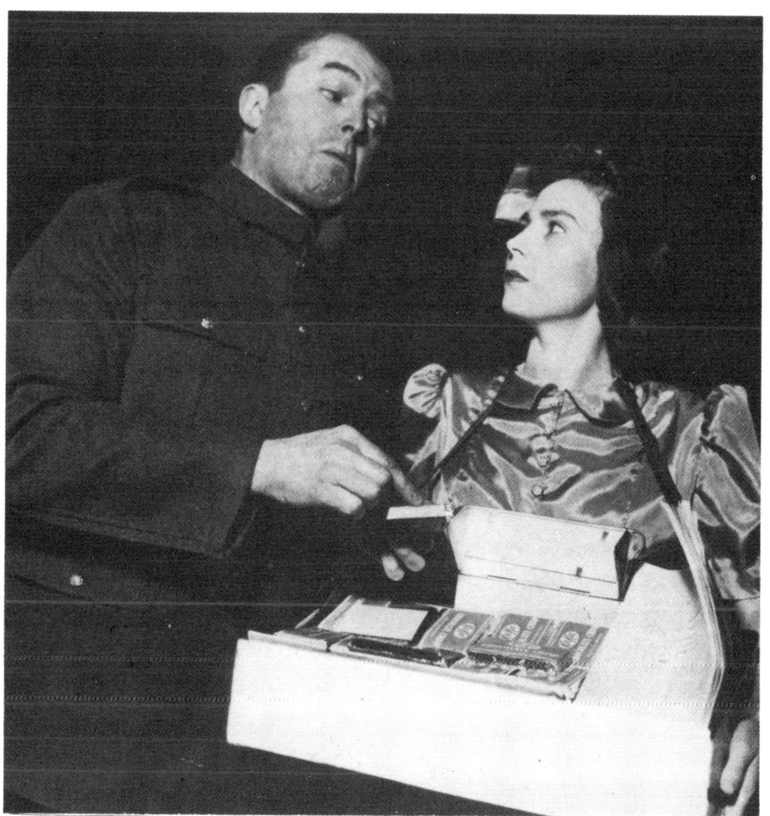

The popular wartime series, Garrison Theatre, *featured Jack Warner as a cockney private and Joan Winters as his "little gel". The programme was responsible for one of the most enduring of all wireless catch phrases; "Mind my bike!"*

own exclusive transmitting frequency. Ironically it was the arrival of war, in September 1939, that accelerated the possibilities of radio for the West Country, as the BBC in London "evacuated" some of its personnel to the provinces. Many of the nation's most popular wartime radio programmes came from Bristol. Wednesday evening symphony concerts came from Colston Hall, and, as already observed, also some editions of *Henry Hall's Guest Night.*

Garrison Theatre was broadcast from the Clifton parish hall, which seems to have been transformed into a mini-Broadcasting

House. Compliments were paid to its basement canteen, virtually a temperance night-club for broadcasters. That radio made you hungry is confirmed by a priority project at the BBC in Whiteladies Road. A canteen building was erected in the back garden in the space of six weeks, ready for the influx from London. Jack Warner, the star of *Garrison Theatre*, entertained his friends with impressions of Maurice Chevalier, and on the air referred to his "little gel", Joan Winters, who also starred in the show. His well-known phrase "Mind my bike!" may have had some radio connections, too, as abundant bicycles were for some time observed in the BBC precincts. Later achieving TV stardom as PC George Dixon, in the series written by Ted (Lord) Willis, Jack Warner also had the rare distinction of being the subject for a full-page cartoon strip in the weekly *Radio Fun* comic.

Concerts were also broadcast from the excellent hall in the CWS building at Broad Quay, Bristol. Up to the 1970s the friendly-looking building, with its four-faced clock tower, was one of the city's best-known landmarks. Further studio facilities were installed at Redland Park Hall, mainly for musical programming. Well-known singers of the period came to this *ad hoc* studio, including Margaret Eaves who was certainly one of the best-known sopranos of the 1940s. Before the war, she had broadcast with Herman Darewski and his band.

As might be expected, though, the splendid precincts of the Whiteladies Road headquarters had the most prestigious programmes, including *Monday Night at Eight*. That wonderful magazine, running up to the nine o'clock news, included Ronnie Waldman's *Puzzle Corner*, plus a mini-mystery called *Inspector Hornleigh Investigates*.

Strange to Relate, another radio programme from Whiteladies Road, offered Mike Meehan's productions of odd tales. The sound effects were reportedly remarkable, and the show was very popular. Mr. Meehan was, of course, an *In Town Tonight* pioneer.

One of the many anecdotes from Bristol wireless days concerned Elizabeth Cowell, who had been one of the pre-war TV presenters. Very shortly before she was about to make a wartime

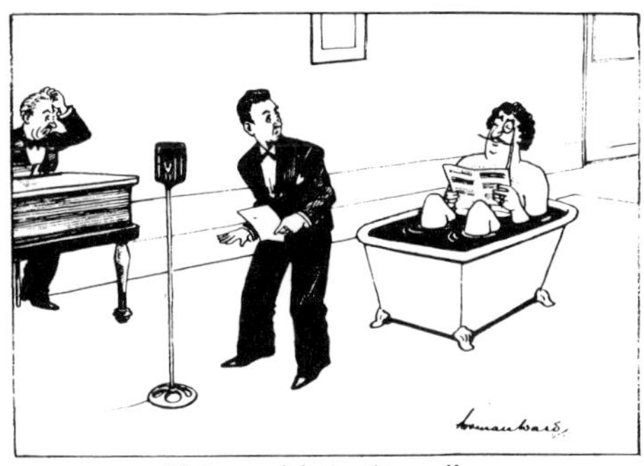

broadcast from Bristol, Elizabeth discovered that she was in the wrong studio. Given the diversity of studio locations around the city, it is surprising that that sort of thing happened so rarely. Accompanied hand-in-hand by a BBC commissionaire, who knew the best short cut to the right studio, Miss Cowell ran through the blacked-out streets of Bristol, arriving at the microphone, as they say, "in the nick of time".

Someone referred to the problems of personal perambulation in the early months of 1940. Icy conditions underfoot meant a certain amount of slithering along the steeper slopes of Clifton, where some of the broadcasters lived. But the newcomers to Bristol knew how to make the best of any tough situation. "Abbie", the secretary to Harry S. Pepper, one of the BBC producers that came to Bristol, recalled that the secretaries from London found their new working environment somewhat spartan and unattractive, though this was hardly surprising, given wartime emergencies in accommodation. "Abbie" told a reporter from the Co-op's *Wheatsheaf* magazine (April 1940):

> But the garden was full of flowers. So we hunted round for jam-jars and filled them with dahlias. At least we had something nice to look at.

During the Blitz, Bristolians might bump into any number of radio personalities. Among many who came to the city to broadcast were Dick Bentley, Dick Francis, George Moon, Binnie Hale, Kay Cavendish, not to mention the guests for *Henry Hall's Guest Night*. So perhaps it is not very surprising that the elegant

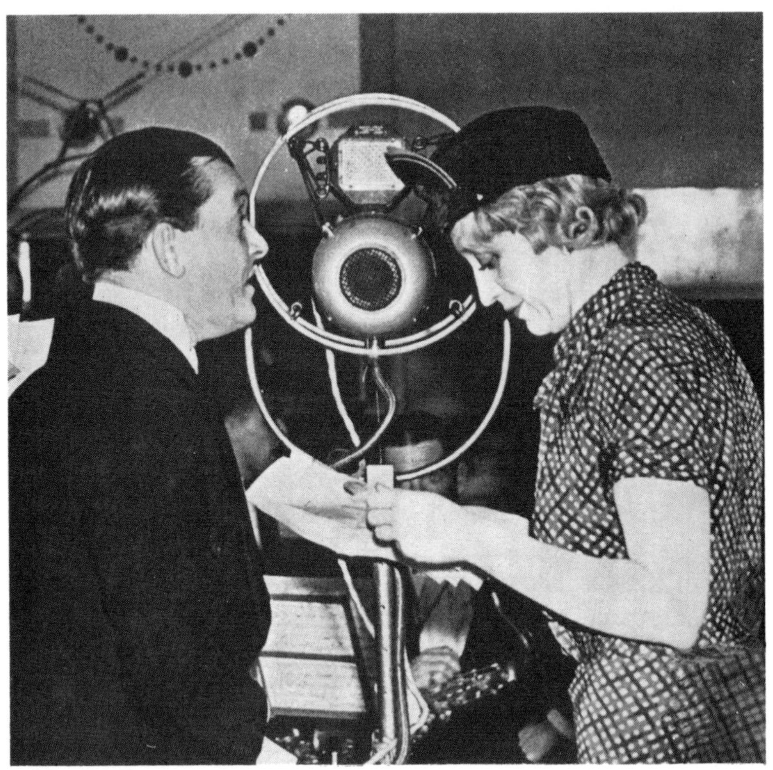

Musical comedy stars Binnie Hale and Bobby Howes, who appeared on Henry Hall's Guest Night.

Broadcasting House in Whiteladies Road became home for a new kind of experimental local radio, "Weekend West", in the late 1960s, prior to the opening of a week-round local station output called BBC Bristol (and on which, incidentally, I broadcast an item on John Wesley's open-air pulpit at Hanham, near Kingswood in east Bristol). Whiteladies Road has become the base for many of radio's most popular programmes, including *Down Your Way*. It might be said that wireless from Bristol has achieved all of the aspirations expressed in the 1920s' "Bristol Radio Weeks". And, despite tight budgets, the BBC no longer has to use jam-jars for its dahlias.

Chapter 16

Gypsy Broadcasters: Unconventional Genius

Given the BBC's interest in gypsies during the 1930s, it would not have been surprising to see a *vardo* (or gypsy caravan) outside the main entrance to Broadcasting House in Portland Place, London. At least, no more surprising than the flat reportedly occupied by Arthur Askey and Richard "Stinker" Murdoch on the roof of Broadcasting House. That bachelor retreat, made famous in the radio programme *Band Waggon*, and later a British film, had at least some of the ecological aspects beloved of the "open-air" broadcasters. A goat provided milk, and reportedly ate unwanted scripts.

Gypsy broadcasters — genuine members of the Romany race — combined those elements of insight, traditional travel background and folk art eagerly sought by radio producers. For that matter, a gypsy in colourful attire provided great potential for publicity photography. The Romany people then, as now, faced problems of social disadvantage, and to a considerable degree gypsy broadcasters attempted to counter the prejudices so often held by *gorgio* (i.e. non-gypsy) listeners. Probably the best known Romany was Gipsy Petulengro, a well-built, abundantly-moustached and dark-skinned man who was as popular with children as adult listeners. His feature in the monthly children's magazine, *Merry Go Round* (Frederick Warne Ltd), was aptly called *Chavvies of The Vardo*, i.e. "Children of The Caravan", and focused primarily on natural history topics. (Incidentally, Richard St. Barbe Baker of *Men of the Trees* fame wrote regularly for this magazine). His literary output was prolific, including autobiographical material and guides to Romany herbal "cures", and yet, like so many other members of his race, Gipsy Petulengro was largely self-educated. In *A Romany Life*, published by Methuen in 1935, he recalled his early childhood in England:

> I was about nine years old and had been in England for nearly two years. I had been quick at picking up the language and could answer my father in English almost as good as his own. But like all Romanys, I knew nothing of reading or writing and I had no knowledge of the alphabet or even what it could mean.

Even so, he was in business on his own account at 11 years of age, developing a range of communication and other skills that were to serve him well in the world of radio. Gipsy Petulengro acquired literacy and a flair for self-expression that soon brought him national recognition.

In Town Tonight — the Saturday night BBC radio interview programme preceded by a loud cry of "Stop!" bringing, so it seemed, traffic to a standstill — took a special interest in Gipsy Petulengro. He was, indeed, one of only two people to appear on the programme more than once, the other being "Rass Prince Monolulu", described as "the famous Abyssinian tipster". This lively character was heaven-sent to cinema newsreel cameramen on great horse-racing occasions. With exotic flair, Rass Prince Monolulu waved his literature towards the bulky tripod-mounted cine cameras and declared, "I've gotta horse!"

Gipsy Petulengro's appearance on *In Town Tonight* had a more therapeutic aspect. He was asked to talk about herbal cures, the British preoccupation with rheumatism being evident in the 1930s as also, alas, in our own times. The BBC's interest in the Romany people properly embraced all true travellers. Among others appearing on the programme were gypsy musicians from Albania, expertly performing on the pan pipes. Lady Eleanor Smith was interviewed about her interest in travelling people, including those who made their livelihood in the circus.

The Gipsy's knowledge of natural life seemed encyclopaedic, though there was one occasion when his knowledge of British agriculture seemed incomplete. Freddy Grisewood, a very popular radio broadcaster, hosted *The World Goes By*, which in format was not dissimilar to *In Town Tonight*. In one of the programmes, Freddy was in discussion with Gipsy Petulengro and, almost as

Amongst this group of interesting characters from a 1930 In Town Tonight *programme can be seen (crouching at the front with an umbrella) the famous racing tipster Prince Monolulu.*

an aside, suggested that British farmers no longer made their own butter. He probably expected Gipsy Petulengro to explain the true situation, but instead the Gipsy seemed merely to give assent to the comment. Even a Romany of the stature of Gipsy Petulengro could not be expected to know everything. Within days of the broadcast, the BBC seemed destined to build its own butter mountain, as diligent farmers from the four corners of the kingdom hastened to assure Freddy Grisewood that butter-making was still in hand down on the farm. They sent samples to prove the point — until the BBC cried "Stop" in the style of *In Town Tonight*, though with expressions of thanks. (The story is also told in Freddy Grisewood's 1950 autobiography, *My Story of the BBC*).

Gipsy Petulengro was crowned "King of the Gypsies" at Baildon, Yorkshire, on 28th August 1937, an event captured by the cinema newsreels. Baildon Moor had long associations with the Romany people, and, according to contemporary reports, some 20,000 people had come to see the ceremony, which was entirely traditional. Gipsy Petulengro led a procession of Romany people, mounted on a fine horse and accompanied by

151

a gypsy prince and princess. Thousands of pigeons were released following the ceremonial crowning, symbolising the carrying of good news to gypsies in every land. As he walked to his throne accompanied by gypsy musicians, wheat was thrown at his feet as a symbol of great fortune, also symbolised by the presentation of a golden cauldron. Like other gypsy broadcasters, he was eager to carry forward the best of the old traditions, increasingly threatened in a world that seemed bent on war. In November 1936 he appeared on television, still an infant medium with a viewing audience almost entirely restricted to the London area. He was perhaps the most colourful representative of the Romany people yet discovered by the broadcasting medium.

His programme on Radio Normandy in the late 1930s had likely appeal to housewives, being broadcast on Friday mornings (10.15am) and including "Luck Charts" and horoscopes. It was sponsored by Skol Healing Antiseptic, and programme promotion emphasised that the broadcaster was a *genuine* Romany. Although Gipsy Petulengro was described as "The Radio Seer", and certainly had no doubt as to the genuine nature of "second sight", one gets the impression that he was most at home in rural surroundings, rather than surrounded by the aloof technology of the studio. In June 1937, a magazine competition offered as its prize an all-expenses-paid trip to London, there to visit Gipsy Petulengro for lunch before enjoying a theatre matinée. Although little, if any, coverage seems to have been given to the subsequent excursion, the encounter must have been unforgettable. Perhaps there was a souvenir package of herbal cures, too.

Another pioneer gypsy broadcaster — and not only in Britain — was the evangelist, singer and writer, Gipsy Rodney Smith, MBE, better known as "Gipsy Smith". Some of his early gramophone (phonograph) recordings pre-date radio broadcasting, and by the 1920s and 1930s a number of Gipsy's Columbia 78rpm records were widely enjoyed. Gipsy's work in radio began before the establishment of the British Broadcasting Corporation in 1927. One of his first broadcasts was from the studios of the pre-BBC British Broadcasting Company in Marconi House at Kingsway in Central London. Gipsy's great friend and occasional

The colourful and flamboyant Gipsy Petulengro who was featured on the front cover of the Radio Pictorial for 18th June, 1937.

accompanist, Harold Murray, was to recall, years later, the somewhat primitive equipment in the spartan studio. Gipsy was told that the box-like microphone could not be moved, raised or lowered, and was invited to stand on a wooden soap-box in order to provide an adequate signal. Accustomed to large audiences — or perhaps smaller groups of students at lectures — Gipsy hardly felt at ease. As Harold Murray wrote, "Gipsy missed his crowd, their laughter and their song. He was worried by the silence of the studio, the necessity of watching the clock — all those strange sensations that must affect every man who has to talk to a great unseen audience".

Although Gipsy Smith, on that early encounter with radio, seems to have suffered something of the emotional let-down known to broadcasters in every generation, he agreed to further broadcasting engagements. When, soon afterwards, he broadcast from the Blythwood studios near Glasgow, a group of volunteers from local churches helped with musical accompaniment. Thereafter Gipsy proved no stranger to the medium, though he did not seek to make a reputation as a radio preacher. His roving itinerary hardly permitted *that*, but one may find, in vintage journals, references to his work in the medium. During the mid-1930s, he broadcast from Wesley's Chapel in City Road, London. During that broadcast the then resident minister, The Rev. George MacNeal, spoke of his own conversion, some 40 years earlier, under the ministry of the gypsy evangelist.

When he visited Australia in 1926, Gipsy Smith found himself involved in one of the most interesting examples of pioneering "religious radio". Gipsy's mission was centred on meetings held in the Sydney Hippodrome, though, as Gipsy's visit was something of a national event, the churches arranged for radio transmissions, some of these being used for local evangelistic efforts (as were the early radio-link transmissions of the Billy Graham Crusades in Britain and possibly elsewhere). Among those using the radio link in this way was a Methodist, The Rev. A.F. Walker, whose congregation — many miles away — listened attentively to the transmission from Sydney, up to the point at which Gipsy made his "appeal". At that point, The Rev. A.F. Walker had the

Gipsy Smith, who preferred speaking to an audience that he could see.

radio signal muted so that he could make his own "appeal", and two-thirds of the church congregation rose to their feet, either to re-dedicate themselves to their Christian labours, or to commit their lives to Christ for the first time. Gipsy Smith remembered the words of the overjoyed minister in his 1932 book, *The Beauty of*

Jesus: "A wave of divine power seemed to grip our hearts", he wrote.

The remarkable impact of this radio innovation was perhaps best summed up by another minister, The Rev. William Taylor:

> Distant? No! A voice right there in our midst, with all its vibrant power and intensity, all its cheering and convincing power. Yes, and with far more than that, for indeed, God was in that voice. Think of it! The Holy Spirit coming to us through the radio, reaching and moving the congregation as never before had we seen it moved. I preached the first service at my church here at Lindfield, thirty years ago. Through all the intervening years, never have there been witnessed in this church such scenes as last Sunday night, as it was our great joy to rejoice in.

Gipsy Smith had so many friends, in high positions as in low, that it is perhaps not surprising that he knew Sir (later Lord) Reith, first and, some would say, greatest Director General of the British Broadcasting Corporation. Sir John was a Presbyterian, and no stranger to the deep issues of religion. Indeed, he was instrumental in encouraging the somewhat hesitant churches in Britain to use the emerging medium, the full story being told in Dr. Kenneth M. Wolfe's excellent study *The Churches and the British Broadcasting Corporation: 1922-1956*, published by SCM. But Gipsy's work for the BBC was necessarily limited, in view of his travels to the USA and elsewhere. However, there are still recollections of Gipsy's quietly-spoken talks from the heart, broadcast in the 1930s. In 1970, Mrs. Winifred Hibbins reported to this writer:

> On a Sunday evening in 1933, my fiancé and I heard Gipsy Smith speak in a BBC radio service, and his message on John 3, 16, brought spiritual stirrings that led to my loved one's conversion soon afterwards. I had been praying for this, knowing that I could never face an "unequal yoke". So my joy was two-fold. A radiant Christian, my husband gave his life for his country early in World War Two, and the knowledge that he is with The Lord, together with the wonderful grace of God, has enabled me to keep going until we see Him face to face. Just one testimony, I am sure, to Gipsy Smith's gift of communicating the Gospel, by the power of the Holy Spirit and with simplicity.

Gipsy broadcast many times whilst visiting the USA where, unlike Britain, churches often had part-ownership in local stations. Indeed, a 1939 radio broadcast from the Church Hill Tabernacle, Buffalo, was recently recalled in a letter to this writer.

Gipsy's final broadcast was made in 1947, shortly before his planned return to the USA — the trip was never completed as Gipsy died on board the *Queen Mary* as it neared New York Harbour. In recent years the recording has been broadcast, and though the talk is of a few minutes duration only, it has a specially appealing quality. In it, Gipsy recalls the words of a farmer, a benediction at the very beginning of his work as an evangelist. The farmer had prayed, "Keep him low, Lord", aware that being in the public gaze brings its own temptations, and problems.

As his final testimony on radio, Gipsy rejoiced that the prayer had been answered in his own life, that he had indeed kept low, and thus been able to point all the better to the Creator.

Best loved of all the gypsy broadcasters was "Romany of the BBC", a Methodist minister (The Rev. George Bramwell Evens) who began his radio career at the BBC's Northern Region studios in Piccadilly, Manchester, in the early 1930s. Invited to participate in the *Children's Hour* output — in which the Northern Region excelled — he chose the name "Romany", rather than assuming the conventional prefix of "Uncle". These were of course the great days of BBC "Aunts" and "Uncles", and "Romany" was fortunate in working with outstanding broadcasters, including Muriel Levy and Doris Gambell.

Romany had written country cameos for the provincial press as well as for the *Methodist Recorder*, based on characters he had known whilst stationed in Carlisle — where, incidentally, he was involved in the building of a new Methodist Hall. Sometimes known as "the tramp" (he always advised that old, drab clothing was best for bird-watching), he was hardly a conventional Methodist minister. Yet such was his popularity that his "flock" would not hear of his leaving ministerial labours when he raised the prospect owing to the demands of broadcasting.

The format of his programme, *Out With Romany*, was a sort of "radio ramble", a wonderful achievement of sound effects, good scripting and sheer enthusiasm. Indeed, when after Romany's death in 1943 a press report explained that the production was entirely studio-based, there was widespread disbelief. Additional realism was provided by Romany's spaniel, Raq, who could be heard giving the occasional growl or bark as his

Romany's famous caravan, or "vardo". After his death it was opened as a memorial to him at Wilmslow, Cheshire.

master and two friends, Muriel and Doris, splashed through a stream. Raq was always a great favourite at "live" appearances, as when Romany was asked to speak at a Sunday School Anniversary. (An extensive feature on Romany appeared in *This England*, Winter 1980).

Romany's books fall into two main categories: the earlier volumes, basically the "country cameos" based on his press features and with plenty of human interest, and the later books, illustrated with black-and-white photography and focusing on aspects of wild life. These later books were written for children rather than for adults. Published long before the BBC became considerably involved in book production, the "Romany" books were not mentioned on the radio, the Corporation carefully avoiding anything that could be interpreted as commercialism. One can only imagine the awesome circulation that would have resulted, though Romany himself was little interested in financial rewards.

The gypsy broadcasters were all "true originals" in the art of radio. No doubt Gipsy Smith would advise you that if you want to learn the art of communication *that really lasts*, you should spend more time reflecting on the wonders of Creation!

Out in the open air by his own camp fire, was the life that Romany enjoyed the most.

Chapter 17

Keep Fit, Keep Faith:
Listen while Jogging

Britain's health — moral and physical — is under close scrutiny, and we may well revert to a two-pronged campaign created by the BBC during the Second World War. This good deed was the work of a Melville Dinwiddie, DSO, OBE, MC, who, whilst having been a minister of the Church of Scotland, found himself in charge of the BBC's operations in Scotland at the outbreak of hostilities. Britons, he thought, needed strengthening for the awesome tasks ahead. So he proposed an early morning programme of "inspired PT", providing useful but not too strenuous exercises that could be undertaken by almost everyone. *The Daily Dozen* was broadcast at 7.15am and was in the charge of a slim 60-year-old, Captain J. Coleman-Smith, one of the first men to qualify as a military physical training instructor — though by no means the last, as any former National Serviceman can confirm. He had served in the army through the First World War, returning to civilian life in 1922, when he became housemaster at Glasgow Academy.

The "stretch and bend" instructions were given to the musical accompaniment of a piano which was strong on the loud pedal. Captain Coleman-Smith had an ear for music, and occasionally broke into a melody for his cheerful instructions. Exercises for ladies were provided by May Brown, a lady of great flair and energy, being (among other specialities) organiser of the Keep Fit movement in Glasgow, secretary of the Scottish Country Dance Society, and member of the National Fitness Council for Scotland. She was also keenly interested in golf and hockey. So

A couple of young wireless enthusiasts from the early days of broadcasting.

these two dedicated broadcasters undertook their early morning rigours at the microphone, offering an example of Scottish firmness and strength. Many of the programmes were pre-recorded, in case of early morning black-out problems. Research suggested that women were far more likely to undertake the exercises than men — indeed, a two-to-one ratio in favour of the ladies is reported. Women, it is said, used the exercises as part of their slimming programme, though, in those days of stringent food rationing, the problem of obesity could hardly have assumed the proportions it now possesses.

To balance the proper emphasis on self-improvement by exercises, the BBC in Scotland proposed an interlude of spiritual self-examination. Thus, *Lift Up Your Hearts* followed *The Daily Dozen* after an appropriate interval, and both programmes were launched on 4th December 1939 and continued throughout the war, the former, indeed, enduring until its replacement by a shorter feature (i.e. with three minutes as compared with the five minutes allotted to *Lift Up Your Hearts*). This brief comment, *Thought For The Day*, has tended to become more a religious — and not specifically Christian — comment on current events. *Lift Up Your Hearts* had, on balance, been more a *retreat* from current news, recalling the transcendent and traditional aspects of the Established Faith. During the war, when the Christian reflections followed so closely the physical training, it was dubbed "Lift Up Your Knees".

The programmes enjoyed considerable popularity, and even if more lethargic listeners merely yawned at the Captain's instructions, they nevertheless heard the underlying message: life is real, life is earnest, and you *can* help keep yourself away from the undertaker. Although "The Radio Doctor" (Dr. Charles Hill, later Lord Hill) and many other experts advised the nation on health care, diet and exercise, it fell to the Scots broadcasters to secure a balance between the physical and the spiritual. Perhaps the programmes might be combined, and returned to radio as "Stretch Your Faith" — inspirational talks to be heard on your portable radio while jogging.

The golden age of the wireless — when radio sets rested majestically on the sideboard — is often remembered as one in which we sat and listened. What better example is there for the veteran knob-twiddler than the early morning exercisers? What better advice for the nation, than that we should "lift up" both our hearts and our spirits in the cause of national renewal?

Who else was on the Wireless?

There hasn't been room, unfortunately, to mention all of the marvellous men and women who kept us entertained on the wireless for so many years, but in this final pictorial tribute, readers might recognise one or two of their own personal favourites ...

During the 1940s, Cheerful Charlie Chester's Stand Easy programme featured "The Amazing Adventures of Whippit Kwick, the cat Burglar". Members of his "Crazy Gang" included Arthur Haynes, Ken Morris, Len Marten, Louise Gainsborough and Ramon St. Clair

Wilfred Pickles pictured with a group of factory workers for a 1947 edition of Have A Go.

Who can forget H-H-Hancock's Half Hour? Here, Tony is at the microphone with Kenneth Williams, Bill Kerr and Sidney James.

Ted Ray and his Ray's A Laugh team, including Kitty Bluett and Kenneth Connor.

Arthur English, "Prince of the Wide Boys". His signature tune was "Powder Your Face With Sunshine".

Spike Milligan, Harry Secombe and Peter Sellers, collectively, of course, The Goons.